MICHIGAN SPORTS TRIVIA

Chip Mundy
and
J. Alexander Poulton

OVER
TIME
BOOKS

© 2010 by OverTime Books
First printed in 2010 10 9 8 7 6 5 4 3 2 1
Printed in Canada

All rights reserved. No part of this work covered by the copyrights hereon may be reproduced or used in any form or by any means— graphic, electronic or mechanical—without the prior written permission of the publisher, except for reviewers, who may quote brief passages. Any request for photocopying, recording, taping or storage on information retrieval systems of any part of this work shall be directed in writing to the publisher.

The Publisher: OverTime Books is an imprint of Éditions de la Montagne Verte

Library and Archives Canada Cataloguing in Publication
Mundy, Chip, 1955–
    Michigan sports trivia / Chip Mundy, J. Alexander Poulton.

Includes bibliographical references.
ISBN 978-1-897277-58-4

    1. Sports—Michigan—Miscellanea.
I. Poulton, J. Alexander (Jay Alexander), 1977– II. Title.

GV584.M5M86 2010   796.09774   C2010-903031-1

Project Director: J. Alexander Poulton
Editor: Michelle Nichol
Cover Image: Football field (Ford Field, Detroit): CC–Creative Commons, © Mrmiscellanious; race car: © Don France Photography; basketball court (Palace of Auburn Hills): © Kevin.Ward; football: © Toddtaulman I Dreamstime.com; baseball glove: © Bobbiholmes I Dreamstime.com; golfer: © iStockphoto.com/Sergey Kashkin; speed skater: © iStockphoto.com/corepics; boxing gloves: © Zedcor Wholly Owned; lacrosse stick: © Hemera Technologies; all other images: © Photos.com.

We acknowledge the financial support of the Government of Canada through the Book Publishing Industry Development Program (BPIDP) for our publishing activities.

Canadian   Patrimoine
Heritage   canadien

PC: 5

Contents

Dedication

For my late father, Charlie, who gave me the love of sports, and my late mother, Beverly, who gave me the love of writing.

Acknowledgments

This book is the result of opportunity, teamwork and friendship—and it's wrapped together by passion. My publisher gave me the opportunity to work on this project, and for that I am grateful and hope that it meets his high expectations. The book was also a team effort, and I appreciate the great work and research by co-author J. Alexander Poulton of OverTime Books. I also was blessed to be paired with a wonderful editor, Michelle Nichol, who did a remarkable job editing and fact-checking the manuscript. And finally, this book could not have happened without friendship. In my lifetime, I have attended hundreds and hundreds of sporting events, mostly in Michigan but not entirely so, and I did so with many different and wonderful people. It would be impossible to name everyone, but if you ever attended even one game with me, know that you're a part of this book, too. I'm passionate about sports in Michigan, and having friends who feel the same way has been one of life's greatest pleasures. I could not have enjoyed sports without friends who feel the same way.

Introduction

There's an old saying: "One man's garbage is another man's treasure." The same could be said about sports trivia; what doesn't matter to one person might be a cherished memory for another, and, really, that's what this book is about: memories, creating them and reliving them.

As you read this book, you're going to recognize some things you already know, like the championship years of the Tigers, Lions, Red Wings and Pistons, and some of the greatest players from those teams. No review of Michigan sports history would be complete without them, but the hope here is twofold: first, to supply stories or information about those times that are not widely known, causing you to say to yourself, "I didn't know that," and second, to stir your memory of a player, game or time, causing you to say to yourself, "Wow, I forgot all about that." Sports trivia can be different to every person, but all sports fans have a thirst for those "little-known facts," with apologies to Cliff the mailman on the television show *Cheers*.

Maybe you've been at a Red Wings playoff game and saw an octopus thrown onto the ice but never really knew how the tradition started, or maybe you've thrown one on the ice yourself. Maybe you've heard about quarterback Bobby Layne leading the Lions to the NFL title in 1953 but didn't know that he reportedly put a curse on the team when he was traded.

This book is going to be heavy on Lions, Tigers, Red Wings and Pistons trivia, and Michigan and Michigan State will get their share as well. But we're not going to overlook golf, auto racing, boxing and the female athletes of the state, either.

Consider it a walk through Michigan's rich tradition of sports, with a little bit of "one man's garbage" sprinkled in with an assortment of "another man's treasures."

Chapter One

The Tigers: A Team for All Ages

Imagine going to a place where your grandfather took your father when your dad was just a kid. And, in turn, if you're lucky, you'll take your son or daughter to the same place. That's what Tiger Stadium was to baseball fans in Michigan, and that's what the Detroit Tigers have been to the state since 1901—a span of five or six generations of baseball fans.

Football may be America's number one sport, but baseball has the longevity and consistency that no other sport can offer. Who hasn't picked up a bat and swung at a pitch? Who hasn't played catch? Baseball is a sport that most people can relate to, and in Michigan, the Detroit Tigers have one of the most loyal followings of any baseball team.

Before the Tigers

Long before the appearance of the Detroit Tigers, the Wolverines were the Motor City's first professional baseball team. After the National League decided to expel the Cincinnati Reds in December of 1880, it was decided at a league meeting that Detroit would be awarded a new franchise. Naming that team proved to be easy, as we all know that Michigan is the Wolverine State, so the new club became the Detroit Wolverines.

The Detroit Wolverines pulled off a successful inaugural campaign by finishing the season in fourth place and making a tidy profit. But, even before the second season began, the club found itself involved in a war with a rival league, the American Association. Players began to leave Detroit to sign more lucrative contracts in the American Association and, as a result, the fortunes of the team on the field floundered.

The Wolverines spent several years in the middle of the standings until the organization purchased an entire team out of Buffalo in order to obtain Dan Brouthers, Hardy Richardson, Jack Rowe and Deacon White. These four players would be the backbone of the team's future, and during the 1886 season, the Detroit Wolverines finished with 87 wins and 36 losses. An excellent season, but the Chicago White Stockings were better, and Detroit had to settle for second place. But the 1887 season was far brighter, and Detroit finished at the top for the first time. However, that was as good as it would get for the Wolverines as fans began to lose interest in the team and players began demanding higher salaries. At the end of the 1888 season, the players were sold off to other teams, and the franchise was sold to interests in Cleveland.

One of the more beloved Wolverines players was Charlie Bennett, a catcher who had both legs amputated after a train accident in 1894. Two years later, the Tigers built a wooden ballpark and named it Bennett Park, located at the corner of Michigan and Trumbull avenues in downtown Detroit. The first game at Bennett Park was won by the Wolverines 17–2 over the Columbus Senators. Starting in 1896 and running through 1927, Bennett threw out the first pitch on opening day in Detroit.

Naming the Tigers

Although the Detroit Tigers franchise was established in 1894, they were still officially called the Wolverines as they played in the Western League. It was only in 1901 that the team officially changed its name to the Tigers. As to how they came to be named the Tigers, there are several legends that continue to float about the pages of history books and in sports bar conversations. Former Tigers manager George Stallings tried to take credit for naming the team, but the Tigers brand appears in newspaper accounts before Stallings was even a manager. Some even said the Tigers got their name because of the orange and black stripes on their stockings. But, as Richard Bak wrote in his book, *A Place for Summer: A Narrative History of Tiger Stadium*, the name more than likely comes from the

Detroit Light Guard military unit, which was more commonly known as the "Tigers." The unit earned several distinctions during the Civil War and the Spanish-American War. It was a journalist from the *Detroit Free Press* who decided to inject a little heroic language into the on-field performance of the Wolverines and began equating the Wolverines with the Tigers. The nickname caught on, and in 1901, the Wolverines received formal permission from the Light Guard to use the name, officially becoming the Detroit Tigers.

Hello, American League!

Because of inclement weather, baseball fans in Detroit had to wait an extra day to see the Tigers make their debut as a charter member of the American League. Finally, on April 25, 1901, the fans got their game, and the Tigers made it worth the wait. A crowd of 10,023 fans made their way to Bennett Park to watch their team play the Milwaukee Brewers, but the Tigers didn't start out so well. In fact, going into the bottom of the ninth inning, Milwaukee had a 13–4 lead. The Tigers eventually made it a one-run lead, and with two runners on and two outs, Pop Dillon hit a two-run double to give Detroit a 14–13 lead on the strength of a 10-run rally in the ninth inning. The double was Dillon's fourth of the game, and through the 2009 season, no Tigers player has been able to hit more than four doubles in one game.

The Suicide of a Manager

In 1902, the Tigers acquired pitcher Win Mercer, who just four years earlier had won 20 games in back-to-back seasons with Washington in the National League. Mercer had slipped in seasons after that but appeared to get his career back on track with Detroit as he had a team-high 15 wins with a 3.04 ERA. Following the season, the Tigers announced that Mercer would become manager in 1903, at a salary of $3800 for the season. Mercer took the Tigers on a three-month barnstorming tour to the west, and the tour finished in San Francisco. On January 13, 1903, the Tigers were in San Francisco, and Mercer left the team at the Langham Hotel and registered at the Occidental Hotel under the name George Murray. There, he wrote several notes and then asphyxiated himself. One of his notes said: "Beware of women and a game of chance." Some historians believe that Mercer had gambled and lost most of the money owed to the players and committed suicide to avoid having to face them. Others blamed the suicide on a relationship with a woman. Nothing is known for sure, and the Tigers were left to find another manager for the 1903 season.

Traded to Pay the Rent

In 1905, the Detroit Tigers were in a very strange predicament. After the team finished their training camp session in Augusta, Georgia, the Tigers management didn't have enough money left to pay for the use of the facilities. Thinking quickly, the Tigers came up with an easy solution. In return for the money owed, they offered their rookie pitcher, Eddie Cicotte, to the local Augusta minor league team. At the time, the arrangement appeared to be a good solution for all parties involved. Cicotte would eventually turn up in Boston, then move over to the Chicago White Sox as one of their ace pitchers who helped them win the World Series in 1917. Cicotte was also one of the eight players who were permanently banned from major league baseball because of the 1919 conspiracy to throw the World Series. However, one cannot help but wonder what path his career might have taken had the Tigers simply paid their rent.

Tragedy Strikes the Cobb Family

We all know the legendary Ty Cobb as one of the greatest baseball players of all time. He had a .367 career batting average, is third all-time in stolen bases with 892 and second all-time with 4191 career hits. His story on the baseball diamond has been told in countless books and articles, but few of these recount the tragedy that rocked his life before he even stepped up to the plate in the major leagues.

Cobb's parents had, by all appearances, a happy marriage, but in the summer of 1905, William Cobb suspected his wife was having an affair. On the night of August 8, William left the house under false pretenses in order to return and catch his wife in the act. Returning to the house a short time later, William crept up to the bedroom window and peered in to see if his wife was with another man.

Meanwhile, terrified that an intruder was outside trying to get in, Mrs. Cobb pulled out her shotgun and shot at the silhouette through the window, instantly killing her husband. She was arrested and charged with murder, but the charges were later dropped.

Just three weeks after the death of his father, Ty Cobb played in his first major league game for the Tigers against the New York Highlanders. "He never got to see me play...but I knew he was watching me, and I never let him down."

Three Pennants in a Row

The Tigers vaulted to the top of the American League in 1907, winning the pennant by 1.5 games over the Philadelphia Athletics. Detroit's opponent in its first World Series—and just the fourth World Series in history—was the Chicago Cubs, who were 107–45 and won the National League by a staggering 17 games. Amazingly, the first game the Tigers ever played in the World Series ended in a tie. The score was 3–3 after 12 innings and declared a tie, and the Cubs swept the next four games to win the World Series.

In 1908, the Tigers repeated as American League champions and finished just a half-game ahead of the Cleveland Naps. Detroit won the pennant on the final day of the season with a 7–0 victory at Chicago behind pitcher "Wild Bill" Donovan. The Cubs were waiting for the Tigers in the 1908 World Series, and again the Tigers failed to beat the National League team from the Windy City. The Tigers did manage to get their first World Series win with an 8–3 victory at Chicago in Game 3, but the Cubs won the World Series in five games. It would be the last World Series championship for the Cubs for at least the next 100 years.

In 1909, the Tigers won 98 games and took their third consecutive American League pennant by 3.5 games over the Philadelphia Athletics. The World Series was to be against the Pittsburgh Pirates, who won 110 games and took the National League pennant by 6.5 games over the Cubs. The World Series was billed as a meeting of the two best players in the game: Tigers outfielder Ty Cobb and Pirates shortstop Honus Wagner. It was a more competitive World Series than the previous two for the Tigers as the teams traded victories in each game. The Tigers won Games 2, 4 and 6 before losing in Game 7 8–0 as Babe Adams was the winning pitcher for the third time in the World Series. As far as the Cobb vs. Wagner angle, Wagner finished with the upper hand individually and teamwise. Cobb batted .231 (6 for 26) with three doubles, five RBIs and two stolen bases, while Wagner hit .333 (8 for 24) with two doubles, six RBIs and six stolen bases.

A New Ballpark

With the exception of Sunday home games in 1901–02, which were played at Burns Park, the Tigers had been playing at the corner of Michigan and Trumbull since the building of Bennett Park in 1896. After the 1911 season, Bennett Park was demolished for a new ballpark on the same site: Navin Field. Perhaps the most prominent change at the new stadium was the playing field itself. At Bennett Park, home plate was located at the same place as the right-field corner in Navin Field. The change was made to help keep the sun out of the eyes of the batters. The first game in the new ballpark was played on April 20, 1912, and the Tigers beat Cleveland 6–5 in 11 innings in front of a crowd of 24,384.

Although renovated a few times, Navin Field would be the home of Tigers baseball through the 1999 season. It was renamed Briggs Stadium in 1938 and Tiger Stadium in 1962 and became known for its flagpole in center field—the only flagpole in fair territory in baseball—and the over-hang in right field that was actually over the playing field. On a high fly ball to right, it was possible for an outfielder to be at the fence, ready to catch the ball, only to see it land in the upper deck.

There was another oddity at the stadium. For years, a sign was posted outside the visitor's clubhouse. It had a simple message: Visitor's Clubhouse—No Visitors Allowed.

The Georgia Peach

After the three consecutive pennants, the Tigers contended only a couple of times in the next 24 seasons. The one real positive was the play of Ty Cobb, known as "The Georgia Peach," and one of the best players in the game. Cobb collected 3900 hits as a member of the Tigers, finishing with 4191 and a career batting average of .367—the best of any player in baseball history. He batted better than .400 three times and won 11 American League batting titles in 12 seasons, including eight in a row.

Cobb was a feisty player whose main asset, other than his hitting skills, was his ability to steal bases. He set a record (later broken) in 1915 with 96 stolen bases and finished his career with 897 stolen bases. He often slid into the bases with his spikes up, and he was not well liked among his opponents and even some of his teammates. But his teammates had his back when Cobb was suspended.

It was May 15, 1912, and the Tigers were playing the Highlanders in New York. A fan, Claude Lueker, had been heckling Cobb for years at Hilltop Park, and Cobb finally broke. He went into the stands to physically confront the fan, who had lost one hand and most of another in a printing press accident. As Cobb continued to beat Lueker and kick him with his spikes, the crowd pleaded for Cobb to stop, to which he reportedly said, "I don't care if he's got no feet."

Commissioner Ban Johnson suspended Cobb indefinitely, and even though many of the Tigers disliked Cobb, they were outraged by the commissioner's actions and went on strike. The team's next series was in Philadelphia against the Athletics. The Tigers scoured the Philadelphia area to find enough players to field a team and offered $10 to each player and $25 to the pitcher, who turned out to be Allan Travers, a 20-year-old who had pitched at St. Joseph's College. Travers was battered for 26 hits as the Tigers lost to the Athletics 24–2. The commissioner reduced Cobb's suspension to 10 days, and the Tigers players returned to the diamond. Travers never pitched again in the major leagues, and he was later ordained into the priesthood. He remains the only Catholic priest ever to play in a major league game.

Cobb, meanwhile, continued his assault on the major league record book. In 1921, the Tigers made him a player-manager, but he could not lead the Tigers to first place. In six seasons as manager, Cobb had a record of 479–444 with a best finish of second in 1923. The Tigers released Cobb after the 1926 season, and he spent the last two seasons of his career with the Philadelphia Athletics.

Mickey Cochrane

After finishing fifth in the 1933 season, the Tigers needed a spark, and they wanted to find it with a new manager. Co-owner Frank Navin wanted to hire Babe Ruth to manage the Tigers, but Navin's partner, Walter O. Briggs, preferred star catcher Mickey Cochrane from the Philadelphia Athletics. In fact, Briggs loaned $100,000 to the Tigers to purchase the contract of Cochrane from Philadelphia, and the Tigers had their first player-manager since Ty Cobb a decade earlier. Not much was expected of the 1934 Tigers, but with Cochrane as the spark plug, the Tigers won the American League pennant. Cochrane was named the MVP of the American League—quite an accomplishment.

In 1935, the Tigers repeated as American League champions, and Cochrane scored the winning run on a single by Goose Goslin in the clinching Game 6 of the World Series against the Chicago Cubs. "It was my greatest day in baseball," Cochrane said in *The Detroit Tigers Encyclopedia*. It made quite an impression on Paul Gallico, the sports editor of the *New York Daily News*. Gallico wrote, "It was something to see, Mickey Cochrane stabbing his spikes into the plate with the winning run and then going mad, like a young colt, leaping and cavorting about, shaking his bare, dark head.... When Cochrane stood on second, a lone figure in white, I have never seen such will and energy from a single person. He had to come home. He willed to come home. I believe if Goslin hadn't hit he would have stolen home from second base."

Things would go quickly downhill after that for Cochrane. He had a nervous breakdown in 1936, and, in 1937, his playing days—and nearly his life—came to an end when he was hit by a pitch by New

York Yankees pitcher Bump Hadley on May 25. The ball hit Cochrane on the right temple, fracturing his skull in three places. He lay near death for days in a hospital before he recovered, but his playing days were over as doctors warned Cochrane that another beaning could end his life.

A year later, Cochrane was fired, but when he was elected to the Baseball Hall of Fame, he went in as a member of the Tigers even though he played just 315 games of his career with Detroit. He had played the first 1067 games of his career with the Philadelphia Athletics, who won three consecutive American League pennants from 1929 to 1931 with Cochrane as their catcher.

Incidentally, on October 20, 1931, a baby boy was born in Spavinaw, Oklahoma, and his father decided to name him Mickey after Mickey Cochrane. That baby was Mickey Mantle.

Mechanical Man

During the Detroit Tigers' glory years of the 1930s, three of their star players had surnames that began with the letter "G": Hank Greenberg, Charlie Gehringer and Goose Goslin. All three would end up in the Baseball Hall of Fame, and they were instrumental in the Tigers reaching the World Series in 1934 and 1935.

Gehringer was the first to arrive. Known as the "Mechanical Man" for the way he made playing second base look so easy, Gehringer played in just a total of 13 games in 1924–25 before settling in as a starter in 1926. He stayed in Detroit for all 19 of his big-league seasons, playing in three World Series and six All-Star Games and winning the American League MVP Award in 1937. Gehringer, who grew up in Fowlerville, about 60 miles from Detroit, finished his career with a .320 batting average and 2839 hits.

Go Green

Hank Greenberg was next, coming to Detroit in 1930 for one game and joining the team as a regular in 1933. Greenberg might be the greatest power hitter in the team's history as he clubbed 306 home runs in his career, including a team-record 58 in 1938, and he had a team-record 183 RBIs in 1937. Six times in his 12-season career with Detroit, he reached at least 125 RBIs in a season and still managed to have a career batting average of .313. Among the first great Jewish athletes to play in the United States, Greenberg missed four years in his prime to enter the service during World War II, and if he had played those seasons, his career records would be even more impressive.

Being Jewish, he was faced with a tough decision in 1934: September 10 was Rosh Hashanah, one of the holiest days of the Jewish calendar, and the Tigers had a game with a four-game lead in the standings. Greenberg played, hit two home runs to help the Tigers win 2–1, and 10 days later he spent

Yom Kippur in a synagogue. Greenberg was not one to turn his back on the Jewish culture.

Greenberg was a two-time American League MVP, winning the honor in 1935 and 1940, and in 1938 he threatened Babe Ruth's single-season record of 60 home runs. He needed just three home runs to beat Ruth with five games left in the regular season, but he didn't get much to hit and was shut out. He walked four times in the last five games of the regular-season finale, causing some to wonder if pitchers avoided pitching to Greenberg so that a Jewish player would not break the sacred record set by Ruth.

Greenberg left the Tigers in early May of 1941 to join the service. His final game was on May 6 at home against the Yankees, and he thrilled the Briggs Stadium crowd by hitting home runs in each of his first two at-bats in a 7–4 victory over the New York Yankees. Tigers fans would not see him in action again until July 1, 1945, when he returned from the war and played for the Tigers against the Philadelphia Athletics on a Sunday afternoon at Briggs Stadium. And Greenberg picked up where he left off, hitting a solo home run in the eighth inning as the Tigers defeated the Athletics 9–5. After a salary dispute prior to the 1946 season, Greenberg's contract was sold to the Pittsburgh Pirates for $75,000, and he played there for one season.

Goose Goslin

The last of the G-Men to arrive in Detroit was Goose Goslin, who spent the first nine-plus seasons of his career with the Washington Senators. He went to the St. Louis Browns for three-plus seasons and returned to Washington for one season before the Tigers acquired him in a trade for John Stone prior to the 1934 season. Goslin spent four seasons in Detroit, reaching at least 100 RBIs in his first three seasons. Goslin is best known for delivering the two-out, run-scoring single that broke a 3–3 tie in the ninth inning of Game 6 in the 1935 World Series, giving Detroit its first championship.

An Ugly World Series

The Tigers got back to the World Series in 1934, and instead of facing the Chicago Cubs or the Pittsburgh Pirates, it was the St. Louis Cardinals who were the National League champions. That Cardinals team was known as "The Gas House Gang" and featured star pitchers Dizzy and Paul Dean. The teams split the first six games, setting up a deciding Game 7 in Detroit with Dizzy Dean on the mound for St. Louis and Eldon Auker for the Tigers. However, the Cardinals spoiled the fun for Detroit by scoring seven runs in the third inning and building a 9–0 lead by the sixth inning. In the top of the sixth inning, Joe "Ducky" Medwick tripled, and his hard slide into Tigers third baseman Marv Owen angered the Detroit fans. When Medwick went to take his spot in left field in the bottom of the sixth inning, the fans pelted him with fruit, bottles and pretty much anything else they could get their hands on. Commissioner Kenesaw Mountain Landis finally ordered Medwick out of the game for his own safety. Since the Cardinals had an 11–0 lead, Medwick left with no argument, and the Cardinals went on to win the World Series.

Winning the World Series

Finishing the regular season with a comfortable lead on the second-place New York Yankees, the Detroit Tigers were the heavy favorite to win the 1935 World Series, but they would have to pull together and play some of their best baseball of the season. Their opponents, the Chicago Cubs, had finished the regular season with a far better record and a winning momentum, going into the World Series with 21 consecutive victories in September— still a league record as of 2009. For Tigers fans, a World Series victory was long overdue. The Tigers had been in the World Series in 1907, 1908, 1909 and 1934 and had lost each time.

The Tigers headed into the World Series with probably their greatest lineup of players, including stars like "Hammerin" Hank Greenberg, Charlie Gehringer, Billy Rogell, Goose Goslin, player-manager Mickey Cochrane and the only 20-game-winning pitcher of the 1935 season, Tommy Bridges. The first two games of the series were to be played before the home crowd at Navin Field. The tension before the start of each game was palpable—Tigers fans did not want to put too much emotion into the series, as they had gotten used to disappointment.

The Cubs managed to win Game 1 on the strength of pitcher Lon Warneke's four-hit shutout. In Game 2, the Tigers answered the Cubs with an 8–3 win before a packed home crowd, but the win was a costly one as they lost the services of Greenberg, one of their best hitters. Greenberg had fractured his wrist when he collided with Cubs catcher Gabby Hartnett after trying to score from first on a single.

As the Series moved to Chicago for Games 3 and 4, the Tigers won both to back the Cubs into a corner, despite the loss of Greenberg. Game 5 brought Cubs pitcher Warneke back on the mound, and he held the Tigers to just one run in a 3–1 victory to keep his team alive. Game 6 was back in Detroit, and the Tigers needed a hero to end the series before their home crowd. With two outs and a man on base, that hero was Goslin, who singled to score Cochrane with the game-winning run.

Even before the Detroit player could cross home plate, delirious fans rushed onto the field in celebration and partying raged through the city until the next day. Tigers owner Frank Navin, who had owned the team for 30 years and had seen his club lose in the World Series so often, was finally able to celebrate a victory. However, just five weeks after the Tigers' championship, Navin died of a heart attack while riding a horse.

A Rookie Beats The Babe and Lou Gehrig

In August of 1937, Tigers rookie catcher Rudy York put on a power display that was unmatched by Babe Ruth or Lou Gehrig. York broke Ruth's record for the most home runs in a month when he hit 18 (Ruth's record of 17 was set in September of 1927), and York had 49 RBIs that month, one better than the record of 48 set by Gehrig.

Incidentally, York's record of 18 home runs in a month was broken in June 1998 by Sammy Sosa of the Chicago Cubs. Sosa hit his 19th home run of the month against the Tigers in Tiger Stadium on June 25, and five days later, he established the record of 20 with a home run against the Arizona Diamondbacks. York's total remained the American League record through the 2009 season.

"I'll Win This One for My Daddy"

Pitcher Bobo Newsom led the Tigers to the World Series in 1940 with a 21–5 record, and Tigers manager Del Baker picked him to pitch Game 1 of the World Series. The Tigers beat star pitcher Paul Derringer and the Cincinnati Reds 7–2. "I feel great over that one because my father was out there watching me," Newsom was quoted as saying in a 1977 *Sports Illustrated* article. Henry Quillen Buffkin Newsom had traveled from his home in South Carolina to Cincinnati to watch his son pitch in the World Series, and he wasn't disappointed. However, the following day, Newsom's father died in a Cincinnati hotel room. A visiting physician said heart problems had killed Henry Newsom, but Bobo thought otherwise. He claimed that his father had died because he had seen his son win a World Series game, and that was all he had been living for.

Newsom started again in Game 5, and he pitched a three-hit shutout in memory of his father as the Tigers won 8–0 to take a 3–2 lead in the World Series. Prior to the game, he promised, "I'll win this one for my daddy." After the game, Newsom said, "I don't think anyone could have beaten me today. It was the game I wanted to win the most."

The Reds won Game 6, and the Tigers turned to Newsom to start Game 7 on one day's rest. Reporters questioned the pitcher before the game and asked if he was going to win Game 7 for his father like he had in Game 5. "Why no," Newsom said. "I think I'll win this one for old Bobo." Newsom held the Reds scoreless over the first six innings as the Tigers clung to a 1–0 lead, but Cincinnati scored two runs in the bottom of the seventh inning for a 2–1 lead, and that's how the game ended. The following season, Newsom was 12–20 for the Tigers with a 4.60 ERA, and he was sold to the Washington Senators for $40,000 prior to the 1942 season.

Newsom had a long career that began in 1929 and ended in 1953, though he pitched only in the minor leagues in the 1949, 1950 and 1951 seasons.

He was a 200-game winner and a 200-game loser, finishing with a career record of 211–222.

The Longest Game

Amazingly, the longest game ever played by the Detroit Tigers ended in a tie. On July 21, 1945, the Tigers and the Philadelphia Athletics played to a 1–1 tie in 24 innings at Shibe Park in Philadelphia. Perhaps the most famous aspect of that game revolves around Tigers pitcher Clyde "Les" Mueller, who pitched a single-game record 19⅔ innings. He allowed only one unearned run and yielded 13 hits with six strikeouts and five walks. He was lifted from the game after walking two batters in a row after getting the first two outs of the inning. Mueller estimated that he threw about 370 pitches in the game, which, after 4 hours and 48 minutes, was eventually called because of darkness.

Prince Hal

Many baseball experts would point to "Prince Hal" Newhouser as the greatest pitcher in Detroit Tigers history. He certainly has the statistics to back up that claim—a two-time American League MVP who finished second another time, Newhouser won at least 20 games in a season four times, was a six-time All-Star and was elected to the Baseball Hall of Fame. However, Newhouser, who grew up in Detroit, has his share of detractors as well. Their main point is that Newhouser's best seasons came during World War II, when many of the top players in the game were in the service, meaning that he did not face the best players of his era, and when he did, he wasn't as effective.

Here are the facts: in 1944, Newhouser won his first American League MVP award, and he won it again in 1945. In 1946, he was second in the voting for the same award. Newhouser also proved to be a big-game pitcher. He won two games in the 1945 World Series, including a complete-game effort in Game 7. In the 1948 regular-season finale, Newhouser was matched with legendary Cleveland pitcher Bob Feller—Newhouser threw a five-hitter as the Tigers beat Cleveland 7–1.

Two No-hitters in One Season

The 1952 season was not a memorable one for the Detroit Tigers, except for the exploits of pitcher Virgil Trucks. That season, Trucks became just the third pitcher in baseball history to throw two no-hitters in the same season.

On May 15, Trucks made his sixth appearance and fifth start of the season at home against the Washington Senators. He pitched a no-hitter with seven strikeouts and one walk, but it wasn't officially a no-hitter until Vic Wertz hit a two-run homer in the bottom of the ninth inning to give Detroit a 1–0 victory with only 2215 in attendance at Briggs Stadium.

Finally, on August 25, Trucks recorded his second no-hitter in a game at Yankee Stadium, and the

Tigers won 1–0. This time, Detroit scored in the top of the seventh inning, so Trucks was able to walk off the field with a no-hitter after retiring Hank Bauer on a grounder for the final out in the ninth inning. Trucks had a solid career, finishing 177–135 with a 3.39 ERA, though the Tigers traded him in a six-player deal after the 1952 season.

Incidentally, Trucks threw four no-hitters during his days in the minor leagues.

The Kid Arrives

Al Kaline was a skinny kid right out of high school when he signed with the Detroit Tigers at the age of 18. And he was a rarity—he never spent a day in the minor leagues, going directly to the Tigers after he signed in 1953. Kaline was a "Bonus Baby," a term used for any player who accepted a signing bonus of more than $6000. Those players had to spend the first two seasons of their careers in the big leagues instead of gaining game experience in the minors. It was baseball's way of trying to limit giving big bonus money to young players. Kaline received a $15,000 signing bonus plus the major-league minimum salary of $6000 for each of his first two seasons in Detroit.

Kaline was mostly used as a pinch-runner that first season. He became a regular in 1954, batting .276. But nothing he did in 1954 suggested the kind of season he had in store in 1955.

All Kaline did in 1955 was collect 200 hits, win the American League batting title with a .340 average, hit 27 home runs and drive in 102 runs. In the process, he became the youngest person ever to win a batting championship, and he did it by one day— Kaline was 20 years, nine months and six days old when he won the batting title; former Tigers great Ty Cobb previously held the record of 20 years, nine months and seven days. Kaline's coming-out party was April 17, 1955, in a game against the Kansas City Athletics at Briggs Stadium. He went 4-for-5 with three home runs and six RBIs as the Tigers thumped Kansas City 16–0. Kaline's three home runs that day came off three different pitchers.

Kaline established himself as a bona fide star, and he eventually became known as one of the greatest right fielders ever to play the game. Twice he was named the American League Player of the Year by *The Sporting News*, he was a 13-time All-Star, he won 10 Gold Gloves and he was elected to the Baseball Hall of Fame the first year he was eligible, in 1980. Kaline finished his career with a .297 batting average with 399 home runs and 3007 hits, nearly becoming the first player in history to total at least 400 home runs with at least 3000 hits. On June 1, 1958, Kaline hit a home run off White Sox pitcher Ray Moore in the second inning, but the game was rained out after 3.5 innings, wiping Kaline's home run off the record book. That home run would have given him 400 for his career.

However, Kaline's 3000th hit could not have been much better—it came on September 24, 1974, off Orioles pitcher Dave McNally in Memorial Stadium in Baltimore. Kaline was born and raised in Baltimore.

Sunday's Hero

They called Tigers outfielder Charlie Maxwell "Paw Paw" because that's the name of the small town in Michigan where he lived. But "Sunday Charlie" was just as appropriate a name for Maxwell, who became known for hitting home runs on Sundays. After he was traded to the Chicago White Sox, Maxwell continued his Sunday punch.

Here is a day-by-day breakdown of Maxwell's 148 career home runs: Sunday (40), Monday (7), Tuesday (21), Wednesday (19), Thursday (13), Friday (22) and Saturday (26).

Trading Managers

The Detroit Tigers and the Cleveland Indians did something in 1960 that had never been done before in baseball and likely will never happen again: they traded managers. On August 3, the Tigers were 44–52 under manager Jimmy Dykes and the Indians were 49–46 under manager Joe Gordon, so Dykes was sent to Cleveland and Gordon came to Detroit. It didn't work. Gordon was 26–31 the rest of the season with the Tigers and did not return to the team in 1961; the Indians were 26–32 under

Dykes, who stayed in Cleveland for the 1961 season as the Indians posted a 77–83 record.

But that wasn't the first unusual trade Cleveland and Detroit had ever made. After the 1959 season, the Tigers traded Harvey Kuenn, the reigning American League batting champion, for Rocky Colavito, the reigning American League home run champion. It is the only time in baseball history that the reigning batting champion was traded even-up for the reigning home run champion.

A Seven-hour Baseball Game

It was a Sunday afternoon at Tiger Stadium, and history was about to be made. The Tigers and the Yankees played the first seven-hour baseball game in history. The date was June 24, 1962, and it started out like it was going to be a slugfest.

The game provided some interesting statistics: both teams used seven pitchers, and Rocky Colavito went 7-for-10 to become the first Tigers player to collect seven hits in one game. Jack Reed, who hit the deciding home run in the 22nd inning, had a unique distinction as well: it was the only home run of his three-year major-league career and accounted for two of his six career RBIs.

Legendary Detroit sportswriter Joe Falls was the official scorer at the game and recounted it in his book, *Joe Falls: 50 Years of Sports Writing*. The game had started at 1:30 PM, and Falls noted that it ended at 8:29 PM. The previous record for the longest game in history was 5 hours and 19 minutes, so the record was not an issue. "I did not want a time of six hours and 59 minutes," Falls wrote. "I wanted the magic figure of seven hours. So I paused for a moment before picking up the microphone in the press box. I cleared my throat a few times, and when I thought enough time had passed, I announced: 'Time of game, seven hours.' Two seasons later, on May 31, 1964, the New York Mets and the San Francisco Giants played a 23-inning game at Shea Stadium in New York. The game lasted seven hours and 23 minutes, breaking the record for the longest baseball game in history.

The Tragic 1966 Season

The Tigers were becoming a solid team in 1966 and posted a decent 88–74 record, but it may have been the most tragic season in team history. Manager Chuck Dressen suffered a heart attack on May 16, and he died three months later. Dressen was succeeded by Bob Swift, who was hospitalized in July with what was later dia-gnosed as lung cancer. Swift died on October 16. Swift had been succeeded by Frank Skaff, who finished the 1966 season before Mayo Smith took over in 1967. Iron-ically, Skaff suffered a fatal heart attack in 1988 while scouting a college game for the Tigers at Towson University.

Is That a Hot Dog in Your Pocket?

One of the funniest and possibly the most embarrassing moment in baseball history happened to Detroit Tigers outfielder Gates Brown during a game on August 7, 1968. Brown was a big 220-pound monster known more for his hitting ability than his fielding prowess, but that didn't matter much as he spent most of career as a pinch hitter. Sitting on the bench suited Brown just fine because he had another hobby that he liked as much as baseball—eating. On that day in August, the Detroit Tigers were playing the Cleveland Indians, and Brown sat in his regular spot in the dugout, not expecting to be put into the game until the later innings. Figuring he had time to kill, he sneaked out of the dugout and went to the clubhouse to grab a snack. Brown ordered two hot dogs and covered them with ketchup and mustard before returning to the dugout with his hands full. It was the bottom of the sixth inning, so he thought he had plenty of time to wolf down his snack before the coach would even consider putting him into the game. But, as soon as he bit into a hot dog, manager Mayo Smith called on him to get up to the plate.

Brown had to get ready fast, but he didn't want to let go of his hot dogs, so he stuffed them inside his uniform and walked up to the batter's box with the warm dogs snuggly packed in his jersey. Brown would later say, "I always wanted to get a hit every time I went up to the plate, but this was one time

I didn't want a hit. Wouldn't you know it, I smacked one in the gap and had to slide into second base head-first." Rounding first base, Brown ran at top speed to turn his hit into a double. The throw came in from the outfield, and Brown had to slide into second with his head down. In his zeal to get to second, Brown forgot that he had two hot dogs stuffed in his jersey, and when he stood up, everyone in the stadium could see just what he had been hiding. The Cleveland infielders burst out laughing once they saw the ketchup and mustard stains that were smeared all over the front of his jersey. "It had to be my most embarrassing moment in baseball," said Brown afterward.

Smith, the manager, had no choice but to fine his player $100 for eating on the bench, but through tears of laughter asked Brown why he had done it. Brown simply replied, "Where else can you eat a hot dog and have the best seat in the house?"

Go Get 'Em, Tigers

In 1967, the Tigers were involved in one of the best pennant races in baseball history as four teams—the Tigers, the Chicago White Sox, the Boston Red Sox and the Minnesota Twins—battled into the final week before Boston won the pennant. The Tigers could have forced a playoff by sweeping a doubleheader on the final day of the season, but they lost the second game of a doubleheader to fall one game short. That stinging defeat stayed with the team all winter, and the Tigers were ready to have a great 1968 season. After losing to Boston on opening day, the Tigers won nine in a row, and they moved into first place for good on May 10. Detroit finished 103–59 and won the American League pennant by 12 games over the Baltimore Orioles.

The city of Detroit was rejuvenated. In the summer of 1967, a race riot had divided the city. The riot began on a Sunday afternoon during a Tigers game, and smoke from fires set in the city could be seen over the left-field roof. By many accounts, the success of the Tigers helped the city recover in 1968. It seemed that every car radio was tuned to the Tigers game, and when the game wasn't on, the radio stations were playing the summer's catchiest song, "Go Get 'Em, Tigers." The 1968 season was one of the best seasons in the team's history.

The Grand Slam Kid

Jim Northrup had grown up in Michigan, and in 1968, he had a flare for hitting home runs with the bases loaded. In fact, in a six-day span in June 1968, Northrup hit three grand slams. On June 24, he became the first Tigers player to hit two grand slams in a single game (just 13 players had done it in major league history through the 2009 season). Five days later, he hit his third grand slam of the season when he connected off White Sox starter Cisco Carlos. Earlier in the season, Northrup had hit a grand slam off Washington reliever Steve Jones, so he finished the 1968 regular season with four grand slams.

But Northrup didn't stop there. In Game 6 of the World Series, he hit a grand slam off Larry Jaster to highlight a 10-run second inning for the Tigers in their 13–1 victory over the St. Louis Cardinals that forced a seventh game.

The 30-game Winner

Denny McLain had a once-in-a-lifetime season in 1968. He posted a 31–6 record with a 1.96 ERA and won both the American League MVP and the Cy Young Award. He was the first pitcher in franchise history to win 30 games in a season and the first pitcher since Dizzy Dean in 1934 to reach that figure. He was 14–4 at home with a 2.47 ERA, and on the road, he was 17–2 with a 1.40 ERA. He was brash and cocky and had the sporting world by the tail.

McLain reached 20 wins by July 27, and after beating the Red Sox on August 16, he was 25–3. It was beginning to look like McLain would reach 30 wins. Finally, on September 14—a Saturday afternoon—McLain went to the mound with a record of 29–5. It was the NBC Game of the Week on television, and Dean was brought in to help broadcast the event. The Oakland Athletics were the opponents, and a young slugger named Reggie Jackson helped spoil McLain's moment by hitting home runs in the fourth and sixth innings. Oakland took a 4–3 lead into the bottom of the ninth, and

McLain had to sit in the dugout and watch his team-mates try to salvage the game and pull out the 30th win for their ace. Al Kaline scored to make it 4–4, and Willie Horton followed with a run-scoring single. McLain charged from the dugout to celebrate his 30th win.

Five days later, McLain pitched on a Thursday afternoon against the New York Yankees, and it would be the last appearance in Detroit for legendary outfielder Mickey Mantle, a player McLain admired. Mantle had 534 home runs, tied for third all-time with Jimmie Foxx, and McLain wanted to see Mantle break the tie. With the Tigers leading 6–1, McLain decided to groove one to Mantle. McLain called catcher Jim Price to the mound and told him to tell Mantle that he was going to let him hit one. Mantle, knowing McLain's eccentric personality, wasn't sure if he should believe him or not, but when the first pitch came down the middle with nothing on it, Mantle knew McLain was serious. Mantle hit a home run, and as he rounded the bases, McLain gave him a wink of the eye.

Fame was fleeting, however, for McLain. He shared the 1969 American League Cy Young Award with Mike Cuellar of Baltimore, but in 1970, *Sports Illustrated* broke a story that McLain had been involved with a bookmaking operation. McLain was suspended until July 1, and after the 1970 season he was traded to the Washington Senators and never regained his form. Later in life, McLain was sentenced twice to prison. In 1985, he was found guilty of federal charges of racketeering, extortion and narcotics and was sentenced to 23 years, but the conviction was overturned in 1987 because of procedural violations. In 1996, McLain was found guilty of conspiracy, theft, money laundering and mail fraud and sentenced to eight years. He served more than six years, and after he was released, he wrote a book, called *I Told You I Wasn't Perfect*, which was a follow-up of his previous book, *Nobody's Perfect*.

Mayo Smith's Gutsy Move

As the 1968 regular season came to an end, it was obvious that the Tigers were going to win the American League pennant and play in the World Series. But manager Mayo Smith had a problem: star outfielder Al Kaline had been injured earlier in the season, and the Tigers were doing fine with an outfield of Willie Horton in left, Mickey Stanley in center and Jim Northrup in right. Kaline was now healthy, but there was no room for him in the lineup. And Smith desperately wanted to get Kaline into his first World Series.

Stanley, an outstanding defensive center fielder and the most athletic player on the team, was going to be the key to getting Kaline into the lineup. Smith's first thought was to move Kaline to third base in place of Don Wert, who batted .200 during the season. But Wert was excellent in the field, and

Smith did not want to disrupt the defense at third base. Smith then had a meeting with Kaline and a few other veterans like Norm Cash, Eddie Mathews and Bill Freehan, and presented them with a solution: Smith would move Stanley from center field to shortstop and bench the light-hitting Ray Oyler, who batted .135 for the season. Kaline would then play right field, and Northrup would move from right to center field. Smith then presented his idea to general manager Jim Campbell, and it was a done deal—it would also be one of the gutsiest moves in World Series history.

Stanley had filled in at shortstop late in the first game of a doubleheader on August 23 and started at shortstop in the second game. He prepared for the World Series by playing shortstop for the final six games of the regular season and finished with two errors in 68 innings. The move worked to perfection. Stanley made two errors during the World Series, but neither one had an impact on the game, while Kaline batted .379 (11-for-29) with two doubles, two home runs and eight RBIs.

Brock Is Out at the Plate

The Tigers and Cardinals had split the first two games of the World Series in St. Louis, and the Cardinals won Games 3 and 4 in Detroit, putting the Tigers in a treacherous three-games-to-one hole. The Cardinals, the defending World Series champions, took the field for Game 5 at Tiger Stadium with a chance to repeat as champions. They started quickly, scoring three runs in the first inning off Mickey Lolich, and it looked like there wasn't going to be any championship in Detroit in 1968. After all, only one team had rallied from a 3–1 deficit to win a World Series, and the Tigers were down 3–0 in Game 5 against the defending champions. But the momentum changed in the middle innings.

Lou Brock was a speedy base runner for the Cardinals, and he had stolen seven bases in the first four games of the World Series. Brock hit a one-out double in the fifth, and when he tried to score from second on a single by Julian Javier, he was thrown out at the plate by center fielder Horton. Brock failed to slide into home, and catcher Bill Freehan successfully blocked the plate. Horton explained how the play happened in *Baseball Digest*. "I read the scouting reports, and Lou had picked up some bad habits since the All-Star break," Horton said. "He'd drift a little bit into bases, and Lou didn't slide at home. The third base coach was also a little relaxed on that play." Also, Brock had been caught attempting to steal earlier in the game, and the Tigers were gaining confidence.

In the bottom of the seventh inning, the Tigers scored three runs to take a 5–3 lead. Mayo Smith again made a right move when he decided to let light-hitting pitcher Lolich hit for himself with one out and nobody on, and Lolich delivered a base hit. Dick McAuliffe singled to right, and Mickey Stanley followed with a walk to load the bases, and Al Kaline then smacked a two-run single in what he called the biggest hit of his career. Norm Cash added a run-scoring single, and Detroit went on to a 5–3 victory to send the World Series back to St. Louis for Game 6.

Mickey Lolich: World Series MVP

While 30-game winner Denny McLain was the Tigers pitcher that everybody was talking about, left-hander Mickey Lolich was the winning pitcher in Games 2 and 5. McLain, who had lost two match-ups with National League Cy Young Award winner Bob Gibson, moved up a day to pitch in Game 6 and benefited from a 10-run third inning to beat the Cardinals 13–1. That set up a classic Game 7 with Lolich on the mound for Detroit, and Gibson taking the mound for St. Louis. Both pitchers were 2–0 in the World Series, and Gibson had the reputation of being the best big-game pitcher in baseball.

It was a classic pitchers' duel through six scoreless innings, and it looked as if the game would turn on one big play. That happened in the top of the seventh inning. After the first two Tigers were retired, Norm Cash delivered a base hit, and Willie Horton fol-lowed with a single to left field. Jim Northrup then drilled a ball to center, and Cardinals outfielder Curt Flood, an excellent defensive outfielder, broke in at first and could not recover as the ball sailed over his head for a two-run triple. Bill Freehan followed with a run-scoring double, and the Tigers had a 3–0 lead on the mighty Gibson and the Cardinals. St. Louis spoiled Lolich's bid for a shutout when Mike Shannon hit a two-out home run in the bottom of the ninth, but Lolich regrouped to clinch the Tigers' 4–1 victory and third World Series championship.

Lolich, named the MVP of the World Series, finished with a 3–0 record and a 1.67 ERA. He threw three complete games and allowed 20 hits in 27 innings with 21 strikeouts and six walks.

7-for-7

Six singles and a double. That's what light-hitting shortstop Cesar Gutierrez did for the Tigers in the second game of a doubleheader on June 21, 1970, at Cleveland. No other Tigers player has ever had seven hits in a game, and Gutierrez, who had 128 career hits and a .235 career average, was about as unlikely as anyone to do it. He singled in the first, third and fifth innings and rapped a double in the seventh. He had a run-scoring single in the eighth inning to make the score 8–8, and he added a single in the 10th. Finally, in the 12th inning, Gutierrez singled after Mickey Stanley hit a home run that broke the tie and gave Detroit a 9–8 victory.

In one day, Gutierrez boosted his batting average from .218 to .249. Just how rare was this feat? Gutierrez became the first player to collect seven hits in seven consecutive at-bats in one game since

Wilbert Robinson did it for Baltimore in the National League on June 10, 1892.

Nineteen-game Losing Streak Ends

From July 29, 1975, through August 15, 1975, the Tigers played 19 games and failed to win any of them, creating the longest losing streak in franchise history. Included in the skid was a nine-game homestand against Baltimore, Minnesota and Texas, and on the night of August 16, the Tigers were staring at a potential 20th consecutive loss.

Right-handed pitcher Ray Bare had an unspectacular five-year career, but on that night he pitched one of the two best games of his career—he had a two-hit shutout against the California Angels as the Tigers ended their 19-game losing streak with an 8–0 victory. It was the first of three career shutouts for Bare, who finished his career 16–26 with a 4.79 ERA.

From Prison to the All-Star Game

It might seem fitting that Ron LeFlore was known for stealing while playing professional baseball—he was known for stealing before he played pro ball, too. LeFlore, who grew up on the mean streets of Detroit, was convicted of robbing a supermarket at age 15, and in 1970, he was convicted of armed robbery and sentenced to the Southern Michigan Prison in Jackson, about 75 miles west of Detroit. Although he had not played organized baseball prior to going to jail, LeFlore signed up to play on the prison baseball team, and it just so happened that a fellow prisoner had an outside contact who knew Tigers manager Billy Martin. Martin agreed to come to the prison and give LeFlore a tryout in the summer of 1973. Martin was impressed, and when LeFlore was eligible for parole that summer, he signed a contract with the Tigers and went to the minor leagues.

Within a year, the Tigers called LeFlore up to the major leagues. Mickey Stanley had broken his hand and the Tigers needed a center fielder, so they decided to see what LeFlore could do. On August 1, 1974, LeFlore made his big-league debut with the Tigers by going 0-for-4 in a game at Milwaukee. By this time, Martin had been fired, and Ralph Houk had taken over as Tigers manager. Houk stuck with the rookie, and LeFlore responded with a decent first season. He batted .260 with two home runs and 13 RBIs in 254 at-bats. But the thing that excited Tigers fans was LeFlore's speed, which he used to steal 23 bases in 32 attempts.

LeFlore opened the 1976 season with a 30-game hitting streak, and the nation was taking notice as he finished the season with a .316 batting average and 58 stolen bases. He was voted to start the All-Star Game in Philadelphia just three years after he was released from prison.

In 1979, the Tigers, desperate for a left-handed pitcher, traded him to the Montreal Expos for Dan Schatzeder, who went 17–21 in two seasons in Detroit. LeFlore led the National League with 97 stolen bases in 1980 and left Montreal to sign with the Chicago White Sox as a free agent prior to the 1981 season. He stole 64 bases for the White Sox in two seasons before he was released after the 1982 season, and he never played again in the majors.

LeFlore finished his career with a batting average of .288 and had 455 stolen bases in 597 attempts.

The Bird

Mark "The Bird" Fidrych was one of the most beloved Tigers players in franchise history. He burst onto the scene in 1976 and quickly became the most popular player in the game. He was successful, but even more than that, he was colorful and fun to watch. While on the mound, Fidrych would appear to be talking to the ball, though he was actually talking to himself out loud to pump himself up. He would clap for his teammates when they made a fine defensive play behind him, and he would get on his knees to manicure the mound when it was needed. Once he even sat down on the mound and took off his shoe to get rid of a pebble that had gotten inside.

Soon, everybody wanted to be at the games pitched by Fidrych, and it reached a fever pitch on June 28 when the Tigers were home against the New York Yankees in a game televised nationally by ABC-TV. Fidrych beat the Yankees 5–1, throwing yet another complete game, as 47,855 fans packed Tiger Stadium. And they would not leave until Fidrych, in his socks, returned from the locker room for a curtain call. The rookie was 8–1, and now the entire nation knew about this phenom called "The Bird," so called because he resembled Big Bird from the children's television show *Sesame Street.*

Fidrych was worth at least an extra 20,000 fans in the seats for every game he pitched, and when the Tigers went on the road, opposing teams hoped that he would pitch so they could fill their ballpark, too. Both of Fidrych's next two starts after the Yankees game were at home, and both times more than 50,000 fans showed up at Tiger Stadium. He was also chosen to start the All-Star Game in Philadelphia, though he didn't fare so well, allowing two runs in two innings and taking the loss as the National League scored a 7–1 victory.

Fidrych didn't let his sub-par performance in the All-Star Game get him down, and he rolled through the rest of the season. He was named the American League Rookie of the Year after finishing 19–9 and leading the American League with a 2.34 ERA and 24 complete games. The Tigers had a bona fide star pitcher for years to come—or at least they thought they did.

In spring training of 1977, Fidrych tore cartilage in his left knee while shagging flies, and he underwent surgery. He returned to baseball on May 27 and pitched a solid game, but things soon took a turn for the worse. On July 12, 1977, he felt something pop in his right shoulder and left the game in the first inning. It would be the final appearance for Fidrych in 1977, and it was the beginning of the end. He was able to start in the 1978 season opener for the Tigers and won it 6–2 with a complete-game performance, but he appeared in only three games in 1978 and four in 1979 as he continued to battle injuries. In 1980, Fidrych started nine games late in the season and was 2–3 with a 5.68 ERA, but he never pitched in the big leagues again.

Fidrych returned to his home in Massachusetts, got married and purchased a farm.

He remained a folk hero in Detroit and returned to the area often, always to a hero's welcome. On April 13, 2009, Fidrych was killed when a dump truck he had been working on fell on him. Details of the accident were never confirmed.

Sparky

As the Tigers fought to get back to contender status in the American League, they did so with a successful manager from the National League. Sparky Anderson was hired to replace Les Moss on June 12, 1979, and he managed his first game for the Tigers on June 14. It was a Thursday night at Tiger Stadium, and the Tigers lost 3–2 to the Seattle Mariners. Anderson managed the Tigers through the 1995 season, winning one World Series title and two American League Eastern Division crowns.

He became the first manager to win the World Series with both an American League team and a National League team, and he was elected to the Baseball Hall of Fame in 2000.

Anderson was popular with the media because of his colorful quotes. Here's a sample of some Sparkyisms:

"I only had a high school education and believe me, I had to cheat to get that."

"Me carrying a briefcase is like a hotdog wearing earrings."

"If you don't like Dave Rucker, you don't like ice cream." (Note: Rucker was 16–20 with a 3.94 ERA in his seven-year career.)

"People who live in the past generally are afraid to compete in the present. I've got my faults, but living in the past is not one of them. There's no future in it."

35–5

By 1984, the Tigers had the nucleus of a winner, and they knew it. But nobody could have predicted the torrid start the team would have in 1984. They won their first nine games of the season, lost a game and won the next seven for a 16–1 record. After another loss, they won three in a row, and then they lost two in a row to drop to 19–4. From there, the Tigers won seven in a row, lost a game and then won nine in a row. It all added up to a 35–5 record through 40 games—the best 40-game start in baseball history.

The highlight of the 35–5 start came in the fourth game of the season when Jack Morris threw a no-hitter against the Chicago White Sox in Comiskey Park on April 7. It was the first no-hitter thrown by a Tigers pitcher since Jim Bunning did it against the Boston Red Sox in Fenway Park on July 20, 1958.

Bless You Boys

It quickly became apparent that the Tigers were a special team in 1984, and a special team needs an identity or a nickname. Television sportscaster Al Ackerman used the phrase "Bless You Boys," about the Tigers, and it stuck. In fact, a song with that title became sort of an anthem for the team. It went like this: "Bless you boys, this is the year, the boys are going for it, Tiger fever is here," and it was played constantly on Channel 4, the home of Ackerman and the station on which the Tigers games were telecast.

The Tigers were never out of first place the entire season, a feat that had not been accomplished since the 1955 Brooklyn Dodgers did it in the National League in 1955. But the one glaring weakness the team had prior to the 1984 season was in the bullpen, and Detroit solved that problem when it traded catcher John Wockenfuss and outfielder Glenn Wilson to the Philadelphia Phillies for first baseman Dave Bergman and relief pitcher Willie Hernandez.

Wockenfuss and Wilson were popular players in Detroit, and the trade, made during spring training just a few weeks before the start of the season, was met with much negative reaction.

Hernandez turned out to be the steal of the deal. He was the closer the team needed, allowing hard-throwing reliever Aurelio Lopez to be the set-up man. Hernandez had an amazing season, appearing in a league-high 80 games with 32 saves and a 1.92 ERA. Hernandez won both the American League MVP and the Cy Young Award as the Tigers took the Eastern Division title with a record of 104–58, 15 games ahead of the second-place Toronto Blue Jays. The Kansas City Royals won the Western Division, but they were no match for the Tigers in the American League Championship Series, where Detroit swept Kansas City in three games to earn a spot in the World Series for the first time since 1968.

"He Don't Wanna Walk You"

The Tigers were heavy favorites to win the 1984 World Series against the upstart San Diego Padres, and the stage was set for Game 5 at Tiger Stadium with Detroit one victory away from ending the World Series.

The Tigers were holding on with a 5–4 lead going into the bottom of the eighth inning, with one out, runners on second and third, and Kirk Gibson coming to the plate. Padres manager Dick Williams signaled for reliever Goose Gossage to intentionally walk Gibson with first base open, but Gossage shook his head no. Willams went to the mound to talk with Gossage, who told his manager that he had had good success against Gibson in the past. "Let's go after him," Gossage said to Williams. "You mean you want to strike him out?" Williams asked. "Yeah," Gossage answered. Meanwhile, Tigers manager Sparky Anderson had picked up on what was transpiring on the mound, and he loved it. "He don't wanna walk you," Anderson yelled at Gibson with a smirk on his face. Anderson swung his hands as if to tell Gibson to swing away, and Gibson smacked a Gossage fastball into the upper deck in Tiger Stadium to essentially wrap up the World Series title for the Tigers.

A Finale to Remember

One of the most exciting late-season stretch runs by the Tigers came in 1987, but it took quite a while to get there. The Tigers stumbled at the start of the season, and after 29 games, they were 10–18 and in sixth place in the American League East Division. However, the Tigers went 60–29 in their next 89 games to move into first place, and it eventually turned into a two-team race with the Toronto Blue Jays. Fittingly, seven of the final 11 games of the season were against the Blue Jays, beginning with a four-game series in Toronto. When the series began, the teams were tied in the loss column, but

Toronto managed one more victory for a half-game lead in the standings. Toronto won the first three games of the series—each of the victories was by one run—to extend its lead to 3.5 games with eight games to play. The fourth game of the series, on a Sunday afternoon in Exhibition Stadium, would be crucial to the Tigers' hopes.

It was September 27, 1987, and through eight innings, the Tigers could not score on Jim Clancy and reliever Tom Henke. The Blue Jays took a 1–0 lead into the ninth with Henke, their closer, on the mound, and Kirk Gibson led off with a game-tying home run, forcing the game into extra innings with a tie score of 1–1. The Tigers kept Toronto scoreless in the bottom of the 13th for a 3–2 lead, and they left Toronto trailing the Blue Jays by 2.5 games with seven to play instead of by 4.5 games with seven to play.

The Tigers had a four-game homestand against the Baltimore Orioles and could only manage a split of the series. Toronto, meanwhile, had a three-game homestand with the Milwaukee Brewers, and Milwaukee helped the Tigers by sweeping the series. Toronto came to Detroit for the final weekend of the season holding a one-game lead. The Tigers needed to win two out of three to create a tie or win all three games to take the division title outright.

The opener was played on a Friday night at Tiger Stadium. Toronto scored three runs in the top of the second, but the Tigers scored two in the second and two in the third and hung on for a 4–3 victory, creating a tie for first place in the division. An unlikely hero in that game for the Tigers was Scott Lusader, who hit a two-run homer in the second inning. It was the first career home run for the rookie, who would play in just 135 games in his five-year career and finish with five home runs. The following afternoon, the Tigers squeaked out a 3–2 victory in 12 innings.

So, on October 4, 1987, the Tigers played Toronto with a one-game lead in the last day of the regular season. Frank Tanana of the Tigers and Jimmy Key of the Blue Jays hooked up in a classic pitchers' duel, and the Tigers won the game and the division 1–0 as Tanana pitched a six-hit shutout. Amazingly, after their 10–18 start, the Tigers finished with the best record in baseball at 98–64, while Toronto had the second-best record in baseball at 96–66 but missed the playoffs because there was no wild card at that time.

The Tigers played the Minnesota Twins, who had an 85–77 record, in the American League Championship Series, but the late-season surge must have taken something out of the team. The first two games of the best-of-seven series were played in Minnesota, and the Twins beat Doyle Alexander in Game 1 and Jack Morris in Game 2. The Tigers won Game 3 in Detroit 7–6 when Pat Sheridan hit a two-run homer in the bottom of the eighth inning with the Tigers trailing 6–5, but the Twins won

Games 4 and 5 in Detroit and moved on to the World Series, where they stunned the St. Louis Cardinals to win the championship in seven games.

The 1987 season was the last truly successful season for the Tigers at Tiger Stadium. They won 88 games in 1988 and finished one game out of first place, but they were eliminated from the race three days before the end of the season. Detroit had just two winning seasons in the 1990s during the final seasons of Tiger Stadium.

Goodbye, Tiger Stadium

It was an emotional Monday afternoon on September 27, 1999, when the final game was played at historic Tiger Stadium. The Tigers beat Kansas City 8–2 as Rob Fick hit a grand slam in the eighth inning that nearly cleared the roof in right field. The starting players wore uniform numbers of former Tigers stars: pitcher Brian Moehler wore number 47 for Jack Morris; first baseman Tony Clark wore number 5 for Hank Greenberg; second baseman Damion Easley wore number 2 for Charlie Gehringer; shortstop Deivi Cruz wore number 3 for Alan Trammell; third baseman Dean Palmer wore number 21 for George Kell; left fielder Luis Polonia wore number 23 for Willie Horton; right fielder Karim Garcia wore number 6 for Al Kaline; and center fielder Gabe Kapler went without a number in honor of Ty Cobb (the Tigers did not have uniform numbers when Cobb played for the team).

Fick, the designated hitter, wore number 25 for Norm Cash. A postgame ceremony was held as many former players ran onto the field from center field and went to their respective positions.

First Game at Comerica Park

After playing on the same site—the corner of Michigan and Trumbull avenues—for more than 100 years, the Tigers moved to Comerica Park for the 2000 season, and the first game had to be one of the coldest days for a game in history. There was an ice storm that morning, and had it been any other game, it likely would have been postponed. It was April 11, 2000, and Brian Moehler, who had started the last game at Tiger Stadium, was the starting pitcher for the first game at Comerica Park. Moehler got the win as the Tigers beat the Seattle Mariners 5–2. Todd Jones closed out the game for a save, just like he did in the final game at Tiger Stadium. The starting shortstop for Seattle that day was Carlos Guillen, who would be traded to the Tigers prior to the 2004 season. Guillen spent the remainder of the decade with the Tigers and appeared in two All-Star games.

Not the Worst Ever

In 2003, the Tigers were not only the worst team in baseball but also some felt they were the worst team in the history of baseball. And as the season progressed, it appeared that the Tigers were going to prove it with their record. The 1962 New York Mets, a first-year team, had established the record for the most losses in a season with 120, and, for most of the season, the Tigers were a threat to lose more than that. They would have to win five of their final six games to avoid losing 120 games and tying the Mets.

The Tigers won two in a row at Kansas City and then returned home for a final four-game homestand with the Minnesota Twins, who had already wrapped up first place in the American League Central Division. The Tigers won the first game of the series 5–4 in 11 innings when Shane Halter hit a walkoff home run, but they lost the next night, again in 11 innings. It was their 119th loss of the season with two games to play.

That Saturday night, history seemed to fill the ballpark when the Twins took an 8–0 lead into the bottom of the fifth inning. The Associated Press sent a bulletin to its member newspapers alerting them of the Tigers' likely record-tying 120th loss. But the Tigers scored one in the fifth, three in the seventh and four in the eighth to make it an 8–8 game, and in the bottom of the ninth, Alex Sanchez scored the winning run on a wild pitch. The Tigers needed one more victory to avoid tying the Mets' record for losing, and that Sunday afternoon at Comerica Park, the Tigers beat Minnesota behind Mike Maroth, who had lost 21 games that season to become the first pitcher to lose 20 games in a season since Brian Kingman of the Oakland Athletics in 1980. Maroth finished 9–21 and the Tigers were 43–119—certainly not good, but not the worst ever.

Magglio's Blast

The embarrassment of the 2003 season forced owner Mike Ilitch to invest in some better players, and he started by signing catcher Ivan "Pudge" Rodriguez, a certain future Hall of Famer. The team improved in 2004 and 2005, but nobody could have predicted what would happen in 2006.

On September 24, the Tigers beat the Kansas City Royals 11–4 to clinch a spot in the postseason. Detroit returned home for its final six games with a 1.5- game lead over the Minnesota Twins, but the Tigers lost their last five games of the season and Minnesota won the Central Division championship by one game. Instead of winning the division and getting the home field advantage in the American League Division Series, the Tigers were the wild card, and they had to play the first two games of a best-of-five series in New York against the powerful Yankees.

New York, which had been in the postseason every season since winning the World Series in 1996, were heavy favorites to beat the upstart Tigers, who many thought would be happy just to have made the postseason. The Yankees beat Nate Robertson in Game 1 and had a 3–1 lead after four innings of Game 2, but the Tigers battled back to win the series and advance to the American League Championship Series against the Oakland Athletics.

The Tigers had little trouble with the Athletics, winning the first two games of the best-of-seven series in Oakland. Detroit returned to Comerica Park, knowing that two more wins would earn the Tigers a spot in the World Series for the first time since 1984. The Tigers won Game 3 behind a gem by Kenny Rogers, but Oakland was not going to go down without a fight. The Athletics took a 3–0 lead going into the fifth inning, but the Tigers scored twice in the sixth, and Magglio Ordonez hit a home run to tie the game at 3–3. The score stayed that way until the bottom of the ninth, when Ordonez hit a blast to left for a pennant-clinching home run, setting off a wild celebration at Comerica Park. It remains one of the most famous home runs hit in Tigers history, and it sent Detroit to its 10th World Series.

Ernie's Emotional Goodbye

One of the most beloved figures in the history of the Detroit Tigers is Ernie Harwell, a broadcaster who joined the team prior to the 1961 season and was the voice of the Tigers until 2002, when he retired. In 1992, however, Harwell did not call games for the Tigers—he was fired because the team wanted to go in a new direction. Fans were irate, and one of the first things new owner Mike Ilitch did in 1993 was bring Harwell back to the fans as a broadcaster. Harwell, who is in the broadcasters' wing of the Baseball Hall of Fame, was so popular with Tigers fans that there is a statue of him just inside the main gate of Comerica Park. Everybody loved Harwell, who was considered one of the most genuinely nice people anyone would ever meet.

On September 3, 2009, Harwell announced that he had terminal cancer. He didn't seem fazed, saying instead, "I think that when I heard the news, that I had this cancer, that I had a feeling of security and serenity...but I had a feeling of acceptance because of my belief in Jesus and the Lord."

Harwell requested one last chance to address the Tigers fans directly, and, of course, management obliged. On September 16, in the middle of the third inning during a game with the Kansas City Royals at Comerica Park, Harwell walked to a microphone that had been placed in the area just behind home plate. It would be his goodbye to the Tigers fans. The speech was short but memorable, and Harwell didn't dodge his terminal cancer. "In my almost 92 years on this Earth, the good Lord has blessed me with a great journey. And the blessed part of that journey is, it's going to end here in the great state of Michigan." Harwell told the crowd that Tigers fans were "the greatest fans of all, no question about that," and his final words were, "thank you very much, and God bless you."

Doctors had given Harwell about six months to live, and he outlasted their prediction by a few months. He died on May 4, 2010, at the age of 92, and at his request, his body was laid in repose at Comerica Park two days later, right in front of his

statue. From 7:00 AM until after midnight, thou-
sands of Tigers fans filed past Harwell, who was
laid out in his casket wearing his trademark Greek
fisherman's cap.

The Tigers were in Minnesota playing the Twins
when Harwell died, and the visitation at Comerica
Park occurred while the team was still on the road.
The Tigers honored Harwell in their first home
game after his death on May 10, when they hosted
the New York Yankees. The Tigers beat the Yankees
that night 5–4, which in itself was somewhat ironic
since Harwell had passed away on May 4, or 5–4.

The 28-out Perfect Game

There was nothing to suggest that anything
special was going to happen on June 2, 2010, when
the Tigers hosted the Cleveland Indians at Comerica
Park. Armando Galarraga, who had started
the season in the minor leagues after a horrible
2009 season, was making just his third start of the
season for the Tigers. But that night, Galarraga was
perfect—except an umpire wasn't.

Galarraga retired the first 26 batters he faced and
needed just one more out to register the first
perfect game in Tigers history and just the 21st perfect game in baseball history. The batter, Jason
Donald, hit a grounder to the right of first baseman
Miguel Cabrera, who fielded the ball and threw to
Galarraga, who was covering first base. Everyone
began to cheer, but the excitement quickly turned
to confusion and frustration when first base umpire

Jim Joyce ruled that Donald beat the throw to first base. Television replays showed that Joyce was wrong, and the out should have been recorded and Galarraga credited with a perfect game. To his credit, Galarraga was able to compose himself, and he retired Trevor Crowe on a ground ball to third base to end the game with a one-hitter.

Cabrera had been jawing at Joyce during the final at-bat, and Joyce had said to Cabrera, "What do you want me to do, just give it to him?" Tigers manager Jim Leyland confronted Joyce on the field for a few moments after the game, and then all parties went to their locker rooms. The first thing Joyce did was request a replay of his call at first base, and to his dismay, he discovered that he had made the wrong call. "It was the biggest call of my career, and I kicked the shit out of it," Joyce said. "I cost that kid a perfect game." Joyce requested a meeting with Galarraga to apologize, and the pitcher reacted with amazing composure. Galarraga said that people make mistakes and added, "I got a perfect game. Maybe it's not in the book, but I'm going to show my son the CD."

The next day was a day game, and Joyce was scheduled to be the umpire behind home plate. As a way to show harmony between the two subjects, Tigers manager Jim Leyland had Galarraga take the lineup card to home plate and shake hands with Joyce, who became extremely emotional at the small round of applause given him by Tigers fans and the forgiveness offered by Galarraga. General Motors awarded Galarraga with a new Corvette, and Galarraga's teammates came up with a name for the gem of a game. They called it the "28-out perfect game."

Chapter Two

Gridiron Heroes

When the New Orleans Saints won Super Bowl XLIV in February 2010, it left the Detroit Lions with a dubious distinction: the Lions are the only NFL team in the National Football Conference that has not been to the Super Bowl. The only other team that has been in existence since Super Bowl I and has not been to the biggest game in the NFL is the Cleveland Browns, in the American Football Conference. Detroit's last NFL title came in 1957, which means anybody who is under the age of 55 has no firsthand recollection of a football championship in the city.

That, however, hasn't killed the enthusiasm for the team in Detroit. It's hard to imagine what type of reaction the city and state would have if the Lions ever made it to the Super Bowl. The team's official fight song, "Gridiron Heroes," would probably be one of the most requested songs on the radio.

The Portsmouth Spartans

The Detroit Lions did not begin as an expansion team; instead, they were a transplanted team. The Portsmouth Spartans, based in Portsmouth, Ohio, played as an independent professional football team in 1929 before spending four seasons in the NFL (1930–33). The Spartans were fairly successful, with a combined record of 28–16–7, but after the 1933 season, the franchise was threatened financially by the Great Depression. A group, led by Detroit radio executive George A. "Dick" Richards, who owned the radio station WJR, bought the team for $7952.08 plus a $15,000 franchise fee and moved it to Detroit. Richards decided to rename the team the Detroit Lions to coincide with the Detroit Tigers baseball team. According to football-almanac. com, Richards said that the lion was the monarch of the jungle, and he wanted the Lions to be the monarchs of the NFL.

The Detroit Lions played their first game on September 23, 1934, and beat the New York Giants 9–0 in front of 12,000 fans at the old University of Detroit stadium. They won their first 10 games, including seven shutouts, but finished 10–3. George M. "Potsy" Clark, who had coached the Portsmouth Spartans from 1931 to 1933, was the Lions' first head coach.

Thanksgiving Day Tradition

In their first season, the Lions hosted the Chicago Bears on Thanksgiving Day, in a game to determine the champion of the NFL's Western Division. The game was broadcast coast to coast on the NBC radio network, and the Bears won 19–16 despite two touchdowns by Detroit's Ace Gutowsky. The Lions have played a home game on Thanksgiving Day every year since that first game in 1934, except for a six-year stretch from 1939 to 1944 when the game was not played because of World War II. Through the 2009 season, the Lions had an all-time record of 33–35–2 on Thanksgiving Day.

Winning the NFL Title

The second Thanksgiving Day game helped put the Lions in a position to win their first NFL title. Detroit was 5–3–2 after losing to the Bears on the Sunday prior to Thanksgiving, and Chicago was due back in Detroit for a rematch on Thanksgiving. Needing a victory to stay in the Western Division race, Detroit beat the Bears 14–2 and then thumped the Brooklyn Dodgers 28–0 in the regular-season finale to finish 7–3–2. Detroit won the Western Division by a slim margin over the Green Bay Packers (8–4) to earn a spot in the NFL championship game against the New York Giants, who had a league-best 9–3 record. The game was played on December 15, 1935, at the University of Detroit stadium, and the Lions jumped all over the Giants with 13 points in the first quarter, en route to a 26–7 victory. Ace Gutowsky and quarterback Dutch Clark scored touchdowns in the first quarter, while Ernie Caddel and Buddy Parker had touchdowns in the fourth quarter.

The Lions' First Star Player

Earl Harry "Dutch" Clark, the first Lions player to be inducted into the Pro Football Hall of Fame, had been the quarterback at Portsmouth and retired from playing after the 1931 season to become the head coach at the tiny Colorado School of Mines. He returned to the team when it was sold to Detroit. The first star player for the Lions, Clark also was the top player on their roster when they won the NFL title in 1935.

Clark spent five seasons with the team and was a consensus first-team all-NFL selection in each of his first four seasons with them. During his Lions career, he was 97-for-198, passing for 1236 yards and nine touchdowns. He also rushed for 2311 yards and 27 touchdowns on 469 attempts and caught 18 passes for 234 yards and three touchdowns. He kicked 12 field goals and booted 56 extra points for the Lions and is considered one of the last great drop-kickers in football.

A New Den for the Lions

After playing for four years at the University of Detroit stadium, the Lions finally got a new home.

In 1938, the team moved into Briggs Stadium, which had been home to the Detroit Tigers since 1912. In their first game in their new home, the Lions defeated the Pittsburgh Steelers 16–7.

A Supreme Effort

The first member of the Detroit Lions to lead the NFL in rushing was Byron "Whizzer" White, who finished with a league-best 514 yards in 1940. White, who two years earlier led the NFL in rushing for the Pittsburgh Steelers, left the NFL after the 1941 season to join the U.S. Navy in World War II. He never returned to football, instead enrolling in law school when he returned from the war, and from April 16, 1962, until June 28, 1993, White served as a Supreme Court Justice.

Wally Triplett

A player taken in the 19th round of the NFL draft doesn't normally get much attention, but when the Lions took Wally Triplett of Penn State in the 19th round of the 1949 draft, it had historical significance. Triplett became the first African American football player to be drafted by an NFL team and play in the NFL. There had been other African American players in the NFL, but they signed out of the All-America Football Conference and were not a part of the NFL draft. Also, although Triplett was the third African American player to be taken in the 1949 NFL draft, he was the first to play in an NFL game. He played two seasons for the Lions and started five games. Triplett's highlight was an 80-yard touchdown run—the only touchdown he would score from scrimmage in the NFL—against the Green Bay Packers, setting a team record for the longest run from scrimmage.

What a Catch!

On December 3, 1950, Cloyce Box, a two-time Pro Bowl receiver, set a Lions record that was still unbroken prior to the 2010 season. He had 302 receiving yards in a 45–21 victory over the Baltimore Colts, catching 12 passes that day and scoring four touchdowns. Preceding the 2010 season, only three others players had accumulated more than 302 receiving yards in a game: Willie "Flipper" Anderson of the Los Angeles Rams (336 yards in 1989), Stephone Paige of the Kansas City Chiefs (309 yards in 1985) and Jim Benton of the Cleveland Browns (303 yards in 1945).

Box played all five of his NFL seasons with the Lions and led the NFL with 15 touchdown receptions in 1952. He also caught a 97-yard touchdown pass from quarterback Bobby Layne in a 34–15 victory over the Green Bay Packers in the 1953 Thanksgiving Day game.

The Greatest Decade

Several NFL teams have been designated the "team of the decade" over the past 50 years. The Detroit Lions could make a case for being the team of the 1950s, as they won three NFL titles and played in a fourth title game. The Cleveland Browns also won three NFL titles during the 1950s and appeared in seven NFL title games, including six in a row, but the Lions were 3–1 against them in championship games. Either way, it certainly was the greatest decade in the Lions' history.

The Lions opened the decade with a 6–6 record but improved to 7–4–1 in 1951 to finish second in the Western Conference. That set the stage for three consecutive first-place finishes, starting in 1952 with a 9–3 record. Quarterback Bobby Layne led the offense that put up 334 points, second highest in the league. He completed 139 of 287 passes for 1999 yards and 19 touchdowns, but he also threw 20 interceptions. Layne was a winner who became known throughout his career as a quarterback who could bring a team back from a late deficit to win.

After starting 1–2, the Lions won eight of their last nine games to tie the Los Angeles Rams for first place in the Western Conference, and a playoff was needed to determine which team would represent the conference in the 1952 NFL title game. The Lions already had beaten the Rams twice earlier in the season, and they knocked off the Rams 31–21 to advance to the NFL title game against the Browns.

The NFL title game was played in Municipal Stadium in Cleveland on December 28, 1952. Layne got the Lions on the board first with a short touchdown run in the second quarter, and star halfback

Doak Walker ran 67 yards for a touchdown in the third quarter to give Detroit a 14–0 lead. Pat Harder added a 36-yard field goal in the fourth quarter as Detroit defeated Cleveland 17–7 for its first NFL title since 1935.

Doran vs. Lahr

In 1953, the Rams were able to gain some revenge on the Lions by beating them twice during the regular season. However, no other team would beat Detroit, who went 10–2 and faced a rematch in the NFL title game against the Browns. This time, the game would be held at Briggs Stadium in Detroit, and Cleveland had just concluded an 11–1 season and was heading for its fourth consecutive appearance in the NFL title game. It was a game to remember, and Layne was about to add to his reputation as a clutch quarterback.

Earlier in the game, Lions tight end Leon Hart had injured his knee and was not able to return, so Detroit had turned to defensive end Jim Doran to take Hart's place. On first down, Layne passed to Doran for 17 yards, and Doran returned to the huddle to tell Layne that he could beat his defender, Warren Lahr, on a deep route. Layne would remember, and he wanted to set up Lahr for the big one. On third-and-10, Layne passed to Doran for 18 yards and a first down and noticed that Lahr was becoming upset. It was the edge Layne was looking for, so he turned to Doran in the huddle and asked his receiver if he could get open.

"Lahr and I had been feuding a bit, you know, like you do in a tough game," Doran said in *NFL Top 40*, a book from NFL Publishing. "He said he was gonna hit me in the mouth. When Bobby called the play, I had to keep from smiling as I lined up. I was right in front of him and when the ball was snapped, I extended my forearm like I was going to block him."

Instead, Doran got about four yards past Lahr, and Layne hit Doran for a 33-yard touchdown pass. Doak Walker kicked the extra point to give Detroit a 17–16 lead with 2:08 left to play in the fourth quarter. On Cleveland's first play from scrimmage, Lions rookie Carl Karilivacz intercepted a pass by star Browns quarterback Otto Graham to wrap up the NFL title for the Lions—their second in a row.

The Magic Is Gone

The Lions earned a third consecutive trip to the NFL title game after posting a 9–2–1 record in 1954 and beat the Cleveland Browns 14–10 in Cleveland in the final game of the regular season. While it was a preview of the NFL title game—for the third year in a row—it was not a preview of how the game would turn out. Graham threw three touchdown passes and ran for three more as the Browns denied the Lions a third consecutive NFL title with a 56–14 victory in Cleveland.

The Lions went 3–9 the following season and reversed their record to 9–3 in 1956, finishing second in the Western Conference and missing the playoffs. Coach Buddy Parker, who had scored a touchdown for the Lions in the 1935 title game, left the team after the 1956 season to coach the Pittsburgh Steelers. He had coached the Lions from 1951 to 1956 and had an overall record of 40–19–1 with two NFL titles.

A Comeback

The Lions had a new coach in George Wilson in 1957 and got right back into the postseason, tying the San Francisco 49ers for first place in the Western Conference with an 8–4 record. The Lions and the 49ers each won their final three games to earn the tie for first place, and they had split two regular-season games, with each team winning on its home field. So, on December 22, 1957, the Lions played in the Western Conference playoff at San Francisco, and it was one of the classic games in franchise history. However, there was a catch—the Lions were without their star quarterback, Bobby Layne, who had broken his leg late in the regular season. Backup Tobin Rote was to start at quarterback for Detroit.

The 49ers jumped on the Lions quickly as quarterback Y.A. Tittle threw three touchdown passes in the first quarter, and San Francisco held a 24–7 lead at halftime. The team locker rooms were close to each other, and the Lions could hear the 49ers yelling and celebrating their good fortune. The noise seemed to fire up the Lions, and they made a stunning comeback in the second half.

After Detroit took the lead in the fourth quarter, San Francisco had four offensive possessions, and all four ended on turnovers (a fumble and three interceptions). Jim Martin added a 13-yard field goal to give the Lions a 31–27 lead, and that's how the game ended.

Another Title

Detroit was in the NFL title game for the fourth time in the 1950s, and for the fourth time, their opponent would be the Cleveland Browns. It turned out to be a rout as Detroit built a 31–7 lead by halftime and crushed the Browns 59–14. Again, Rote was stellar, completing 12 of 19 passes for 280 yards and four touchdowns.

It was the last hurrah in the 1950s for the Lions, but it was their brightest decade. Eight players from those three NFL championship teams were later inducted into the Pro Football Hall of Fame: quarterback Bobby Layne, defensive backs Jack Christiansen and Yale Lary, linebackers Joe Schmidt and Frank Gatski, running backs Doak Walker and John Henry Johnson and defensive lineman Lou Creekmur.

The Curse of Bobby Layne

Layne was demoralized after missing out on the 1957 championship. He had always been a winner. During his days as quarterback for the University of Texas, he was the star player on the team and led his group to the 1946 Cotton Bowl Classic title. Putting up great numbers in college secured him a top spot in the draft. Although the Chicago Bears drafted Layne in 1948, it was with the Detroit Lions that he would make a name for himself in more ways than one.

During his time with the Bears, Layne was relegated to third-string quarterback. Unhappy with his position on the bench, he tried to engineer his own trade to the Green Bay Packers. This managing of the team's business did not sit well with the Bears' general manager, and Layne was traded to the New York Bulldogs. With the Bulldogs, Layne got his wish and was made the starting quarterback. Unfortunately for Layne, despite his individual brilliance, the team managed to win only a single game that season. After one season, Layne was traded to the Lions for defensive end Bob Mann.

Although he'd had a solid career with the Lions, after the 1957 championship, Layne was disgruntled, and after Tobin Rote led the team to the title, management questioned the wisdom of keeping Layne on the roster. Seeing that the team could win without Layne, management decided that it was time to trade him while he still had value. In 1958, he was traded to the Pittsburgh Steelers, who were coached by the same Buddy Parker who had coached Layne and the Lions to back-to-back NFL titles earlier in the decade. This trade, however, did not sit well with Layne, and he was widely reported to have said that the Lions would not win the championship for 50 years.

Since that fateful day, the Lions have cobbled together the worst record in the NFL, managing to make it into the playoffs only nine times and winning only one game in the postseason. Also, the 2008 team became the first in NFL history to finish a season with a disastrous 0–16 record—exactly 50 years after the Layne trade.

Thanksgiving Day 1962

The Green Bay Packers of the 1960s are considered one of the greatest dynasties in the history of the NFL, and some people believe the 1962 team was the best of all the Packers teams. But on Thanksgiving Day in 1962, the Packers could do nothing to stop the defensive line of the Lions—the original "Fearsome Foursome" of tackles Roger Brown and Alex Karras and ends Darris McCord and Sam Williams. Earlier in the season, Green Bay had edged Detroit 9–7 on a 27-yard field goal by Paul Hornung, and it was a game the Lions felt they should have won. So when Green Bay arrived at

Tiger Stadium with a 10–0 record, the Lions were ready—and so were the "Fearsome Foursome."

The Lions sacked Green Bay quarterback Bart Starr 11 times in a 26–14 victory over the Packers. It was the only game Green Bay would lose all season as the team went on to win the NFL title. "Brown led a vicious, unstoppable Lion rush, which completely overpowered, then brought to frustration and collapse, a Packer offense which stood as the very best in pro football," sports writer George Puscas wrote in the *Detroit Free Press*.

Ironically, Karras of the Lions and Hornung of the Packers were both suspended for the entire 1963 season by NFL commissioner Pete Rozelle for betting on NFL games and being associated with gamblers. Five other Detroit players were fined for betting on the 1962 NFL championship game.

Sweetan to Studstill

Unless the length of an NFL field is changed, nobody will ever break the record held by former Lions quarterback Karl Sweetan and wide receiver Pat Studstill. On October 16, 1966, Sweetan and Studstill hooked up for a 99-yard touchdown pass in a 45–14 loss to the Baltimore Colts at Memorial Stadium in Baltimore. It was just the third time in NFL history that a pass play had covered 99 yards. Through the 2009 season, it had happened 11 times, but only once for the Lions. It's a record that can be tied, but can never be broken.

Introducing Number 20—Lem Barney

There are not very many uniform numbers that
carry as much history through as many different
players as number 20 for the Detroit Lions. Although
cornerback Lem Barney was not the first player to
wear the number 20, he was the first to make it
famous, and his first NFL game was one to remember. Barney was Detroit's second-round draft choice
out of Jackson State in 1967, and the Lions' first
game that season was against the defending NFL
champion Green Bay Packers and standout quarterback Bart Starr. Barney started the game, and Starr
was anxious to test the rookie, so his first pass went
in Barney's direction. Barney intercepted the pass
and ran it 24 yards for a touchdown. Barney finished with 10 interceptions in his rookie season,
including three returned for touchdowns, and he
was named the NFL Defensive Rookie of the Year.

Spending all 11 of his NFL seasons with the
Lions, Barney made the Pro Bowl seven times. He
finished with 56 interceptions in 140 games and
returned seven for touchdowns. As of 2010, Barney
still holds the franchise record for the most yards on
interception returns, with 1077. He was inducted
into the Pro Football Hall of Fame in 1992.

Five to Nothing

After winning the NFL title in 1957, the Lions did
not return to the postseason until 1970, and in 1967,
the Lions hired former star linebacker Joe Schmidt to

coach the team. It took two seasons for Schmidt to make the team a winner, but in 1969, the Lions posted a 9–4–1 record, and in 1970, they went 10–4 to make the playoffs. Detroit was 5–4 after a loss to the Minnesota Vikings on November 15, but they ran off five consecutive victories over the San Francisco 49ers, Oakland Raiders, St. Louis Cardinals, Los Angeles Rams and Green Bay Packers to squeeze into the playoffs as a wild card. Their reward was a divisional playoff game against the Dallas Cowboys at the Cotton Bowl in Dallas, and the streaking Lions came up short in a game that had the unusual final score of 5–0.

A first-quarter field goal and a fourth-quarter safety were all that Dallas was able to do that day against Detroit, which had just 168 yards of total offense. Still, the Lions had a chance to win the game late in the fourth quarter. Bill Munson had replaced Greg Landry at quarterback, and the Lions were able to get into Dallas territory late in the game. Earl McCullouch, one of the fastest players in the game, got open around the Dallas 20, but Munson's pass was high and went off McCullouch's fingers, allowing Mel Renfro to intercept the pass for Dallas. It would be more than 10 years before Detroit would get back to the playoffs.

Death on the Gridiron

It was late in the fourth quarter at Tiger Stadium on October 24, 1971, when tragedy struck the

Detroit Lions. Detroit trailed the Chicago Bears 28–23 and put in the two-minute drill, which meant inserting another receiver in the game. Chuck Hughes trotted onto the field but never trotted off. Hughes went deep over the middle, but the pass, which dropped incomplete, was intended for another receiver. As Hughes jogged back to the Lions' huddle, he collapsed on the turf and died. It was determined that Hughes had suffered a heart attack, and his family had a history of heart problems. It remains the only on-field death in the history of the NFL. Hughes was a little-used receiver, catching only 15 passes in his five-year career. The Lions retired the number 85 worn by Hughes.

The Detroit Wheels

If you don't remember the Detroit Wheels, don't feel too bad. They were forgettable, but still, they are a small part of Michigan's football history. The Wheels played in the short-lived World Football League in 1974. The team played its home games at Rynearson Stadium on the campus of Eastern Michigan University in Ypsilanti, about 30 miles west of Detroit. They even hired Eastern Michigan coach Dan Boisture, which was a disaster. The Wheels opened on July 10, 1974, with a 34–15 loss at Memphis, and they returned home to lose to Florida 18–15 in front of 10,631 curious football fans. The team lost its first 10 games before beating Florida 15–14 in Orlando for the only win in franchise history. The Wheels played two more games and moved to Charlotte before folding after one game. The World Football League folded in the middle of the 1975 season.

The Death of a Coach

After Joe Schmidt resigned as head coach of the Lions after the 1972 season, the team hired a man with a winning background—Don McCafferty, who had coached the Baltimore Colts to victory over the Dallas Cowboys in Super Bowl V. But tragedy struck on the eve of training camp in 1974, and McCafferty died of a heart attack while mowing his lawn and moving sand in the backyard of his suburban Detroit home. McCafferty, who was 53 at the time of his death, had led the Lions to a 6–7–1 record in his first season on the sidelines. Rick Forzano, an assistant coach on McCafferty's staff, took over as head coach for the 1974 season.

Saying Goodbye to Tiger Stadium

With a new home beckoning the Lions, they played their final game at Tiger Stadium on Thanksgiving Day in 1974. The Denver Broncos defeated the Lions 31–27, and Lions running back Leon Crosswhite became the final NFL player to score a touchdown in Tiger Stadium when he found the end zone on a one-yard plunge in the fourth quarter. It was the second—and last—touchdown of Crosswhite's career.

A Domed Home

After playing in the city of Detroit since 1934, the Lions moved to Pontiac, about 30 miles north, to play in the Silverdome, which had an air-supported roof. It was built in 23 months for a cost of about $55.7 million, and the Lions played their first game there on August 23, 1975, in a preseason game against the Kansas City Chiefs. It wasn't until the third week of the regular season that the Lions played an official game at the Silverdome, and it came in front of the bright lights of *Monday Night Football*, with legendary announcer Howard Cosell on hand to watch the Lions play the Dallas Cowboys. Dallas spoiled the party with a 36–10 victory. After four field goals in the first half, Detroit Lions running back Dexter Bussey scored the first touchdown at the Silverdome when he caught a seven-yard pass from Greg Landry and scored.

The Second Number 20—Billy Sims

It took a lot of faith for the Lions to issue a jersey with number 20 on it after the career of Lem Barney, but in 1980, they gave the number to running back Billy Sims, their first-round draft choice who had won the Heisman Trophy at the University of Oklahoma. The Lions had the first pick overall in the draft after going 2–14 in 1979, and Sims was too tempting to pass up. It didn't take him long to make an impression on the Lions. In his first NFL game, Sims scored three touchdowns and rushed for

153 yards on 22 carries as the Lions defeated the Los Angeles Rams 41–20 at Anaheim Stadium in California. He finished his rookie season with 1303 yards rushing with 13 touchdowns, and he also caught 51 passes for 621 yards and three touchdowns.

Sims did even better in 1981, rushing for 1437 yards and 13 touchdowns, but he was only able to play in nine games in 1982 and finished with 639 yards. He topped the 1000-yard barrier again in 1983 with 1040 yards, but a major knee injury in 1984 ended his career. In 60 games with the Lions, Sims gained 5106 yards on the ground with 42 touchdowns, and he caught 186 passes for 2072 yards and five touchdowns. The Lions made the playoffs twice during his brief career, and he played in three Pro Bowl games.

Another One Bites the Dust

When the Detroit Lions started the 1980 season 4–0 with rookie running back Billy Sims leading the way, the team got a little overconfident. Defensive back Jimmy "Spiderman" Allen did a cover of Queen's "Another One Bites the Dust," and it got quite a bit of play on the airwaves. The 4–0 start turned into a 7–7 record, and even though the Lions won their last two games of the season, it wasn't enough to get them into the playoffs. In the end, it was Allen and the Lions who ended up biting the dust.

The Super Bowl Comes to Chilly Pontiac

The windchill dipped below zero on January 24, 1982, when Super Bowl XVI was played at the Silverdome in Pontiac. An ice storm slowed traffic on the highway, and media members got off their chartered buses and walked the remaining mile to get to the game on time. It was the first game played at a cold-weather site, but the weather did not affect the game inside the climate-controlled Silverdome. San Francisco 49ers quarterback Joe Montana was named the MVP of the game after a 26–21 victory over the Cincinnati Bengals.

Back in the Playoffs

In 1982, a players' strike shortened the regular season to nine games. The Lions started 2–0 before the strike interrupted the season after the second game, and it did not resume until November 21. After the strike, the Lions were unable to find the success they had started the season with and lost their first three games and five of the first six. Still, going into the regular-season finale against the Green Bay Packers at the Silverdome, the Lions had a chance to play in the postseason. Eight teams were going to make the playoffs from each conference, and Detroit needed to beat the Packers and have the San Francisco 49ers beat the Los Angeles Rams to make it to the postseason.

The Lions' game ended first, and it was a beauty. Green Bay had taken a 24–20 lead late in the third quarter, and the Lions' Rob Rubick, who had not touched the football all season, entered the game and lined up in the backfield. Quarterback Eric Hipple surprisingly handed off to Rubick, who worked his way into the end zone for a one-yard touchdown run, and the Lions held on for a 27–24 victory. Although Rubick, a tight end, played seven seasons for the Lions, it was the only rushing attempt of his NFL career.

There was still the game between the 49ers and Rams to monitor, and several thousand fans stayed at the Silverdome to watch the finish on the big screen. The fans cheered as the 49ers edged the Rams 21–20 to put the Lions in the playoffs for the first time since the 1970 season. The Lions, who made the postseason despite a 4–5 record, traveled to Washington, DC to play the Redskins in the wild-card round of the playoffs. Washington shot to a 24–0 lead at halftime and defeated the Lions 31–7, and the Redskins went on to win the Super Bowl.

"My Prayer Was Answered"

Despite a 1–4 start in 1983, the Lions got back to the playoffs and traveled to San Francisco to play the 49ers in the divisional round. Detroit had won the NFC Central Division with a 9–7 record, marking the first time the Lions had finished the regular season in sole possession of first place since 1954. The game was played on New Year's Eve, but after the game, the Lions were in no mood to party.

Star running back Billy Sims helped keep the Lions in the game as they rallied from a 17–9 deficit to take a 23–17 lead. A touchdown pass by 49ers quarterback Joe Montana gave San Francisco a 24–23 lead, but the Lions were in a position to win the game. All they needed was to have reliable placekicker Eddie Murray make a 44-yard field goal with five seconds remaining in the game. Murray, nicknamed "Steady Eddie," had already made field goals of 21 and 54 yards in the game.

Prior to the kick, television cameras showed Lions coach Monte Clark with both hands to his mouth in prayer, but Murray's kick barely sailed wide right, leaving the 49ers with a slim 24–23 victory. Clark was crushed but could not help but deadpan an answer when he was asked about his prayer. "My prayer was answered," Clark said. "The answer was, 'no.'" The Lions would not return to the playoffs until 1991.

The Michigan Panthers

Nine years after the World Football League tried and failed to establish a second professional football league in the United States, the United States Football League began play in 1983. Once again, Michigan had a team, and instead of being located in Ypsilanti, the team—called the Michigan Panthers—played in the Silverdome, the same home as the Detroit Lions. And, unlike the Detroit Wheels, the team was a winner, and the Panthers quickly developed a cult following.

The Panthers won their first game 9–7 against the Birmingham Stallions but lost their next three, offering little hope that the team would be a championship contender. But seven consecutive victories put the Panthers in the hunt, and they finished their first regular season under coach Jim Stanley 12–6—good enough for first place in the Central Division. The Panthers had plenty of star power, starting with wide receiver Anthony Carter, who had been a huge fan favorite while playing at the University of Michigan. The quarterback was Bobby Hebert, who would later play for the New Orleans Saints, and placekicker Novo Bojovic was a fan favorite from Central Michigan University. On defense, John Corker led the way with an incredible 28 quarterback sacks.

As the division champion with the second-best record in the league, the Panthers hosted a playoff game against the Oakland Invaders. A crowd of 60,237 fans showed up at the Silverdome to watch the Panthers top Oakland 37–21 and earn a spot in the inaugural USFL championship game.

The opponents were the Philadelphia Stars, who had a 16–3 record, and the championship game was played at a neutral site—Mile High Stadium in Denver. The Panthers appeared to have the game locked up with a 17–3 lead after three quarters, but

Philadelphia staged a comeback with 19 fourth-quarter points. The Panthers won the game when Hebert threw a 48-yard touchdown pass to Carter with 3:01 left to play in the fourth quarter.

The following season, the Panthers struggled to a 10–8 record in the regular season, but it was good enough to send the team to the postseason once again. Michigan had to travel to the Los Angeles Coliseum to play the Los Angeles Express. Only 7953 fans showed up for the game, and they saw a classic. The game was tied 21–21 at the end of the fourth quarter, and it wasn't decided until the third overtime, when Mel Gray scored a touchdown and Los Angeles beat the Panthers 27–21. Gray would later become an excellent return man on kickoffs and punts for the Detroit Lions. The Panthers merged with the Oakland Invaders for the 1985 season, and the USFL folded at the end of that same season.

The Third—and Greatest—Number 20

If the 1950s were the greatest decade for the Detroit Lions—and they were—the 1990s would have to qualify as the second-best decade. The reason is simple—running back Barry Sanders, who was chosen second overall in the 1989 NFL draft and went on to become the greatest player in franchise history. Oh yes, he wore number 20, like Lem Barney and Billy Sims before him.

Sanders was an electrifying runner who won the Heisman Trophy while at Oklahoma State. He wasn't big, but he could stop on a dime, change directions and elude a defender all in one motion. And he was an instant success, just like Sims and Barney had been. Sanders finished his rookie season with 1470 yards and 14 touchdowns, was named the NFL Offensive Rookie of the Year and went to the Pro Bowl, something he did in each of his 10 seasons in the NFL.

Thumbs Up

After losing their opening game to the Washington Redskins 45–0 in 1991, the Lions went on a five-game winning streak. However, in typical Lions fashion, the team lost three of their next four games and took a 6–4 record into their home game against the Los Angeles Rams. It was during that game that the season took a tragic turn.

Offensive lineman Mike Utley was attempting to throw a block on a pass play when he went down onto the Silverdome turf. He knew something was wrong and lay motionless as doctors worked on him. Eventually, Utley was strapped to a stretcher and removed from the field as the fans watched in silence. As the stretcher neared the end zone, Utley managed to raise one hand and put one thumb up to reassure the crowd.

Utley had suffered a spinal cord injury that left him paralyzed, but the tragedy energized his teammates and the entire state of Michigan. "Thumbs Up" was the Lions' rallying cry for the rest of the season, and they not only beat the Rams 21–10 that day, but they went on to clinch their first postseason victory since the 1957 NFL championship game.

Utley was able to turn a negative into as much of a positive as possible. He started the Mike Utley Foundation in January 1992 to help find a cure for spinal cord injuries and to help fund selected research.

More Barry

As the 1990s progressed, the Lions made the playoffs five more times but never won another postseason game. And Barry Sanders continued to amaze football fans with his fancy moves and sensational statistics. The Lions made the playoffs in 1993 and 1994, only to lose to the Green Bay Packers both times.

Sanders topped 1100 yards in each of his 10 seasons with the Lions, and he enjoyed his best season in 1997 when he became just the third player in NFL history (after O.J. Simpson and Eric Dickerson) to reach 2000 yards rushing. Amazingly, Sanders had just 53 yards after two games in 1997, but he didn't fall below 100 in any game the rest of the season. He reached 2000 yards on December 21 at home against the New York Jets in a game the Lions needed to earn a spot in the playoffs. He finished the season with 2053 yards, and center Kevin Glover, maybe Sanders' best friend on the team and one of the team's best blockers, pointed out that the number was ironic—Glover wore jersey number 53.

On the eve of training camp in 1999, Sanders shocked everyone when he decided to retire. He didn't call a news conference, he just issued a statement: "The reason I am retiring is very simple. My desire to exit the game is greater than my desire to remain in it." When Sanders retired, he was just 1458 yards short of Walter Payton's NFL record for career rushing yards. He finished with 15,269 yards and 99 touchdowns, and he was the NFL MVP in 1997.

Barry Sanders was the greatest Lions player of all time, and it's doubtful that the management will ever give another player the chance to wear number 20.

A Painful Turning Point

In the final game of the 2000 regular season, the Lions were at home against the Chicago Bears, needing a victory to guarantee them a spot in the playoffs. Chicago, at 4–11, didn't pose too much of a threat to the Lions, who were 9–6 and had won four of their previous six games. It was Christmas Eve, but Santa Claus was definitely not in the Silverdome that day.

The Lions took a 10–0 lead in the first quarter before Chicago staged a comeback, leading 13–10 going into the fourth quarter. The teams traded leads until Jason Hanson kicked a 26-yard field goal for Detroit to make it 20–20 with 1:56 to play in the fourth quarter. The Bears finally had former Michigan State placekicker Paul Edinger attempt a 54-yard field goal with two seconds to play, and Edinger made it to cancel the Lions' postseason plans.

The defeat put a lot of things into motion for the Lions. Two weeks later, the Lions hired former linebacker and television analyst Matt Millen to be president and CEO of the team. Millen decided to fire interim head coach Gary Moeller, a former University of Michigan head coach, and hire Marty Mornhinweg for the position.

Had the Lions won and made the playoffs, Moeller would have had a 5–2 record as interim coach and gotten the team into the postseason. Would he then have been retained as coach? And, if that had happened, would owner William Clay Ford have created the positions of president and CEO of the club and hired Millen?

Back in Downtown Detroit

The Detroit Lions went home in 2002—home to downtown Detroit with the construction of Ford Field, across the street from Comerica Park, which was the home of the Detroit Tigers. The final game at the Silverdome in Pontiac was played on January 6, 2002, against the Dallas Cowboys. The Lions, who had started the 2001 season 0–12, defeated the Cowboys 15–10 to conclude their final season in the Silverdome 2–14. Johnnie Morton scored the last touchdown in the Silverdome when he caught the game-winning 16-yard pass from quarterback Ty Detmer in the fourth quarter.

The Lions played their first preseason game on August 24, 2002, against the Pittsburgh Steelers, and the first regular-season game was held on September 22, 2002, against the Green Bay Packers. It was the Lions' first official NFL game in downtown Detroit since the 1974 Thanksgiving Day game against the Denver Broncos. Green Bay spoiled the opener, beating the Lions 37–31, but Az-Zahir Hakim scored the first touchdown at Ford Field when he returned a punt 72 yards for a touchdown in the first quarter. Detroit's first victory at Ford Field came the following week when the Lions defeated New Orleans 26–21.

Joey

After their 2–14 finish in 2001, the Lions had the third overall pick in the NFL draft. Desperately needing a quarterback, the Lions chose Joey Harrington out of Oregon, and it turned out to be a big mistake. Harrington started in the first regular-season game at Ford Field. He struggled to complete passes, and by the end of his second season with the team, fans and the media were beginning to wonder if he had what it took to be successful in the NFL.

Harrington showed some improvement in his third season, completing 56 percent of his passes for more than 3000 yards with 19 touchdowns and 12 interceptions. But that was good as he was going to get, and in May 2006, the Lions traded Harrington to the Miami Dolphins for a draft pick. Harrington never made it big in the NFL, but there is one sore sidenote to this story for Lions fans—on Thanksgiving Day in 2006, Harrington returned to Ford Field as a starter for the Miami Dolphins, and they defeated the Lions 27–10.

Steelers Win at Home in Detroit

On February 6, 2006, Ford Field might as well have been the home field for the Pittsburgh Steelers. It was Super Bowl XL, and the Steelers overran Ford Field with their fans as Pittsburgh defeated Seattle 21–10. It was a homecoming for Steelers running back Jerome Bettis, a Detroit native who was playing in his final NFL game. With Pittsburgh about a four-hour drive from Detroit, and Seattle maybe a four-hour plane ride, Ford Field seemed to be 90 percent in favor of the Steelers.

Fire Millen!

As the first decade of the 21st century moved on, there became one constant rallying cry among Lions fans: "Fire Millen!" It seemed that everyone except Lions owner William Clay Ford wanted to see Millen fired from his posts as president and CEO of the Lions. Finally, two games into the 2008 season—with the Lions 0–2, naturally—the team fired Millen. During his time as the president and

CEO, the Lions had a record of 31–83, easily the worst in the NFL over that time period.

0 –16

As the 2008 season unfolded, it became obvious that it was going to be another long season for Lions fans. But, at some point, the team was going to win, right? No NFL team had ever had an 0–16 record (the Tampa Bay Buccaneers were 0–14 in 1976 when the NFL had a 14-game schedule), and the Lions had started the 2001 season 0–10 before winning two of their final six games. But in 2008, the unthinkable happened, and the Lions did finish 0–16. The main culprit was the defense, which finished last in the NFL in points per game given up with 32.3. In fact, the most points the Lions scored in a single game in 2008 was 25, and if the Lions had scored 25 points in each of their games, they would have finished 2–13–1. Head coach Rod Marinelli was fired after the season.

Ironically, in the 2008 preseason, the Lions had posted a 4–0 record and were the only undefeated team in the NFL—proof that preseason results don't mean anything.

Finally, a Win!

On September 27, 2009, the Lions ended a 19-game losing streak by beating the Washington Redskins 19–14 at Ford Field under first-year coach Jim Schwartz. The Lions had a 13–0 lead at

halftime and held on against the sluggish Redskins, who put coach Jim Zorn on the hot seat
a week later when they hired Sherman Lewis to
call their offensive plays.

Chapter Three

Hockeytown

Throughout Detroit's rich tradition with the Red Wings, there have been many up times and some down times. The worst times came in the 1970s and early 1980s, around the time the team moved from historic Olympia Stadium to Joe Louis Arena. The Red Wings were playing poorly, and the crowds at Joe Louis were so sparse that a car was given away at every home game in an attempt to entice fans to attend the games. However, with the arrival of Steve Yzerman in 1984, the team began to see some success, and with the success, the fans turned out at Joe Louis Arena. And by the mid-1990s, when the team was on the verge of winning back-to-back Stanley Cups, Detroit called itself "Hockeytown"—the word was even written across center ice at Joe Louis Arena. Tickets became nearly impossible to get, as the Red Wings annually became one of the top draws in hockey. Other cities have called themselves "Hockeytown," too, and obviously there can be no correct answer as to which city deserves the moniker. Just don't tell that to Red Wings fans.

The Winged Wheel

On May 15, 1926, Detroit was awarded a franchise in the National Hockey League, and four months later, the Victoria (British Columbia) Cougars were sold to a group from Detroit. The team moved to the Motor City and kept the Cougars nickname. However, they were not able to play home games in Detroit right away, so the team had to play across the Detroit River in Border Cities Arena in Windsor, Ontario. Today, the rink is known as Windsor Arena. The team finally found a permanent home in 1927 with the construction of Olympia Stadium on Grand River Avenue, and the name Cougars was changed to Falcons after a newspaper promotion in 1930.

In 1932, a James Norris bought the team, and he was instrumental in renaming the team the Detroit Red Wings. Here is how Bob Duff explained it in *Total Hockey: The Official Encyclopedia of the National Hockey League*:

"Norris had been a member of the Montreal Amateur Athletic Association, a sporting club with cycling roots. The MAAA's teams were known by their club emblem, and these Winged Wheelers were the first winners of the Stanley Cup in 1893. Norris decided that a version of their logo was perfect for a team playing in the Motor City, and on October 5, 1932, the club was renamed the Red Wings."

Coach Adams

It took the Detroit franchise only one year to find its long-term coach. Jack Adams, who retired as a player after the 1926–27 season, was hired to coach the Cougars for the 1927–28 season, and he remained the Detroit coach through the 1947–48 season. Although his overall record was 413–390–161, the stats are a bit misleading. With Adams as the coach, the Red Wings reached the Stanley Cup finals in 1934 and won the title in both 1936 and 1937. Detroit would reach the Stanley Cup finals four times in the next 10 seasons, winning the Cup in 1943 but losing in 1941, 1942 and 1945. After he retired, Adams became the general manager of the Red Wings for the next 15 seasons, and during that time, they won the Stanley Cup four times, in 1950, 1952, 1954 and 1955.

In 1974, the NHL announced that the Jack Adams Award would be given annually to "the NHL coach adjuged to have contributed the most to his team's success."

The Longest Game in NHL History

The Red Wings' first hockey game of the 1936 playoffs was against the defending Stanley Cup champion Montreal Maroons in a best-of-five series. Maroons goaltender Lorne Chabot and Red

Wings goaltender Normie Smith were both having one of their best games of the season. Pelted with a constant barrage of shots, the goaltenders did everything but stand on their heads to stop the shots that came their way.

The first period ended with no score on the board, as did the second period, and when the final buzzer sounded in the third, both clubs were still deadlocked with no goals. The teams returned to their dressing rooms before the start of the first extra period, hoping to end the game in the early stages of overtime.

The score stayed the same through the first and second overtimes, then into the third, fourth and fifth, until the game reached the sixth overtime period at two o'clock in the morning. Radio broadcasters announcing the game began joking that the Montreal Forum staff should provide beds for the remaining fans.

Although the goaltenders deserve accolades for their efforts in keeping the game scoreless, it was a rookie Detroit forward who would be remembered as the player who ended the longest game in NHL history. Mud Bruneteau had been called up to the Red Wings just two weeks before the start of the playoffs and was still getting used to the pace of the big leagues when he was thrown into his first NHL playoff game. But, being a rookie on the team, he knew the coaches were watching, and he could not afford to show any signs of weakness.

In the last few minutes of the sixth overtime period, Detroit forward Hec Kilrea gained possession of the puck and ripped a shot from about five meters away in front of the net. The puck sailed off the blade of a stick, hit a Maroons defenseman and ended up dangerously in front of Chabot, with no Maroons defensemen around. Seeing the puck laying out in the open, Bruneteau rushed to the net and took a wild stab at it. His stick connected, pushing the puck past a startled Chabot and into the back of the net.

The crowd paused, not knowing whether to boo the Red Wings for beating their team or to cheer them for finally putting an end to the game at 2:25 AM. As Bruneteau celebrated his goal, the Maroons slowly made their way off the ice, despondent that they had lost such a lengthy battle. Smith faced 90 shots and Chabot 68 in 176.5 minutes of play. The previous record for the longest NHL game took place in 1933 between the Boston Bruins and the Toronto Maple Leafs, ending at the beginning of the sixth overtime period.

Bruneteau's overtime heroics secured him a spot on the team, and the Red Wings used the momentum of that game to win the series over the Maroons and eventually win the first Stanley Cup championship in franchise history. No teams have since played a longer game in the history of the league.

The Incredible Playoff Collapse

When the Detroit Red Wings finished the 1941–42 regular season with a losing record of 19–25–4, there was little hope that they would make it far in the playoffs. But the hockey gods smiled upon the Red Wings as they got past the Montreal Canadiens and the Boston Bruins to make it into the finals against the Toronto Maple Leafs.

All the papers in Toronto predicted an easy victory for the Leafs, as did many of the Leafs players in the dressing room before the game. The gambling types had Toronto as 8–5 favorites to take the series in convincing fashion. Aware of the gap between his team and the Maple Leafs, Detroit coach Jack Adams knew that his team had one advantage over their opponents—heart.

The Red Wings came out fighting in the first game of the series, pummeling the Leafs into submission with their aggressive physical play. Detroit forward Don Grosso put the game away in the third period with his second goal, setting the score at 3–2 and leaving the Leafs rattled.

After the game, Toronto head coach Hap Day tried to explain to the media what had happened to his club. "There's nothing wrong with our club physically. It's a question of whether or not we've got the stuff that champions are made of. That wasn't hockey out there—it was a fair display of hoodlumism, Detroit's stock in trade."

After Game 1, the Red Wings believed they could win the Stanley Cup. For Game 2, the Wings applied the same strategy, and it worked. The Leafs could not mount any significant opposition to Detroit's heavy hitters and lost 4–2. After the game, Detroit was overflowing with confidence, while the Leafs were left with blank stares on their faces.

"We outfought them, outhustled them and should have beat them 7–3," Adams said.

"Those Leafs will know they had their hides blistered when they get through this series," power forward Sid Abel said. The Red Wings players felt they already had the Stanley Cup in their hands; the remaining games were simply a formality.

If the Leafs did not win Game 3, then any hopes of coming back in the series would effectively fly out the window because no team had ever come back from a 3–0 series deficit in the history of the NHL—or any other professional sport, for that matter. The Leafs took an early 2–0 lead, but the Red Wings came back to win the game 5–2. The Leafs appeared dazed and confused after the game, looking for some way to explain the devastating loss.

"Detroit is unbeatable," said Toronto goaltender Turk Broda, obviously frustrated at his team's inability to solve the Red Wings' brutal attacks. "They're too hot, and they can't seem to do anything wrong." This was exactly the mentality the Red Wings had wanted to place into the minds of

the Leafs, and now they were just one win away
from the Stanley Cup.

Game 4 was intensified when, frustrated at a few
supposed bad calls against the Wings, Detroit forward Eddie Wares directed a volley of verbal assaults
at referee Mel Harwood, who promptly handed him
a 10-minute misconduct penalty. Just a few seconds
later, Harwood spotted Detroit with too many men
on the ice and called a two-minute penalty. Adams
sent Grosso off to serve the penalty, and as he skated
to the box, he dropped his stick and gloves at
Harwood's feet in protest over the call.

Things got worse when the final buzzer sounded
with the Leafs edging out Detroit 4–3. Fuming over
the sudden turn of events, Adams jumped the referee, who was settling the final game stats in the
penalty box, and the two began trading punches.
Seeing the coach fighting for their team, the Detroit
fans got in on the melee and began attacking the
ref. The situation deteriorated when the crowd tried
to attack league president Frank Calder, but the
police jumped in just in time to avoid a catastrophe.
Adams was given a fine and suspended from the
playoffs indefinitely. The coach refused, in his colorful manner, to abide by the ruling of the league.
"They can't keep me out of Maple Leaf Gardens. I'll
buy my way into the place," he said defiantly.

In Game 5, the Leafs outskated the Red Wings on
every level, winning with a score of 9–3. It appeared
that the Wings had exhausted themselves in the

previous games and had simply run out of gas. Detroit employed a different tactic in Game 6 and tried to beat the Leafs at their game by skating hard, but Leafs goaltender Turk Broda put on a stellar performance and shut out the Red Wings. The final was 3–0 but, more importantly, the Leafs had come back from a 3–0 deficit in the series to force a seventh game for the Stanley Cup.

Some 16,218 fans jammed into Maple Leaf Gardens on April 18, 1942, hoping to see their team mark its place in the history books. Over the noise of the crowd, the first whistle could barely be heard as the referee called the players over for the opening faceoff. But the building suddenly went quiet at the 1:44 mark of the second period when Detroit's Syd Howe scored to put the Wings up 1–0. The tension in the building was palpable, as the Leafs could not get a puck past Johnny Mowers in return. The Wings were just 20 minutes away from the Cup.

At the start of the third period, the Red Wings kept pressuring the Leafs' defense, but Toronto forward Sweeney Schriner broke through the Wings' line and managed to tip in a shot to tie the game at 1–1. The Red Wings' bench sunk even further into despair when the Leafs popped in two more goals.

As the buzzer sounded and the Leafs celebrated, Adams said, "Hap did a great job. Toronto deserved to win, I guess. But I think they were a little bit lucky." It had been a tough series, one in which both teams were left with an equal number of injuries, but the Red Wings had the biggest injury of them all—a spot in the history books as the only team ever to lose a 3–0 series lead in the Stanley Cup finals.

The First Howe

Gordie Howe is certainly the best player named Howe to ever wear the winged wheel, but he wasn't the first. In fact, when Syd Howe retired the summer before Gordie Howe arrived for his first training camp, Syd was the all-time leading scorer in NHL history. But he is remembered even more for one incredible game that happened on February 3, 1944. Syd Howe, who had been a member of Detroit's championship teams in 1936, 1937 and 1943, scored six goals in a game against the New York Rangers. No other Detroit player has ever managed to equal the feat.

Mr. Hockey

To compare the play of Gordie Howe to anyone else does a disservice to a man who had talent and a style all his own. During his prime, there was no player on the ice like him. He could score goals in all sorts of ways, play a good defensive game and, if things got a little rough, finish his own fights. He won the scoring title four years in a row, the Art Ross Trophy as the league's top scorer six times, and the Hart Trophy as the league's most valuable player six times. He was named to the All-Star team a record 21 times and held all the league's top scoring records until Wayne Gretzky came along. Even at the age of 41, considered old by hockey standards, Howe continued to produce, scoring 44 goals and 59 assists to break the 100-point mark for the first time in his career.

However, playing at such an intense level for so long took its toll on Howe's body, and at the end of the 1971 season, he retired from professional hockey. The normal Hall of Fame inductee waiting time was waived, and Howe was fast-tracked into the Hall in 1972.

But Gordie Howe could not stay away from hockey for long and, at the age of 45, he joined the new World Hockey Association. He quickly regained his form and scored 100 points in the 1973–74 season. After six full seasons in the WHA, he returned to the NHL and played a full 80-game season with the Hartford Whalers. He contributed a respectable 15 goals and 21 assists at the age of 51 before retiring again in 1980. He played regular professional-level hockey for over five decades, six if you included a 40-second shift with the Detroit Vipers of the International Hockey League at the age of 69. Gordie Howe truly lived up to the name of Mr. Hockey.

The Near Death of Gordie Howe

After Gordie Howe joined the Red Wings in 1946, he became a fixture on the team, known for his intense, physical style of play on the ice. But on

March 28, 1950, at Detroit's Olympia Stadium, the great legend almost lost his life.

Playing the rival Toronto Maple Leafs in the opening game of the 1950 playoffs, the Red Wings had fallen behind 3–0 by the midway point of the second period. Taking up the cause of getting back into the game was Howe's spec-ialty, and as Maple Leafs captain Ted Kennedy carried the puck into the Detroit zone on a rush, Howe saw his moment.

The Toronto captain crossed into the Red Wings zone with Howe and defenseman Jack Stewart following close behind. While Stewart continued with the direct line of attack, Howe swung out and cut across at an angle to head Kennedy off. Out of the corner of his eye, Kennedy spotted the speedy Howe coming in for the check and managed to step out of the way at the last moment to avoid getting plastered to the boards.

What happened next is still up for debate— Kennedy maintained throughout his career that when Howe missed the check, he tripped and flew into the boards. Howe remembered Kennedy's stick catching him in the face before he crashed into the boards. Whoever is right doesn't really matter; what matters is that Howe hit the boards at full speed, headfirst.

A collective cringe traveled through Olympia Stadium as the fans watched their beloved Howe lying on the ice, unconscious with blood streaming from his nose and a gash above his eye. He was immediately placed on a stretcher and rushed to the closest hospital, while his teammates had to continue with the game. At the hospital, it was instantly apparent that Howe's condition was serious, if not deadly. He had broken his nose, smashed his cheekbone, scratched his right eyeball, suffered a severe concussion, experienced swelling of the brain and suffered possible brain damage. A brain surgeon was quickly called in, and emergency surgery was performed on Howe to remove fluid that was putting pressure on his brain.

While Howe recovered in the intensive care unit, Detroit papers began a war of words with Toronto, accusing its captain, Ted Kennedy, of deliberately attempting to injure their star player. But while Detroit papers screamed bloody murder, Red Wings players came to the defense of Kennedy.

"What happened was that as Kennedy saw Howe coming at him, he jumped out of the road, and just then Howe lost his balance and went into the boards," rookie Red Wings forward Max McNab said. "Of course, in those days there was no such thing as television replay to check it out, so everybody had his own version and, naturally, the Detroit people had it in for Kennedy. To hear some of them talk, Kennedy had given our guy a vicious backhander."

Twenty-four hours after the accident, Howe's condition was still listed as serious, but he was out of danger and headed for recovery. "We were a mighty sick bunch all the way to (Detroit's playoff base in Toledo, Ohio)," said coach Tommy Ivan in Stan Fischler's book, *Detroit Red Wings: Greatest Moments and Players*. "I've never seen any of the boys that low before. There wasn't one of us who thought about going to bed until we found out that Gordie was okay."

When word of the successful surgery reached the Red Wings, they returned to action against the Maple Leafs with renewed passion after their opening 5–0 loss. The Red Wings used Howe's recovery from the brink of death as motivation and dispensed with the Leafs in seven hard-fought games.

The next challenge for the Howe-less Wings was the New York Rangers in the Stanley Cup final. The series went to another seven games and then into double overtime before Wings forward Pete Babando put a backhand shot into the top left corner of the net, sending Olympia Stadium into a wild frenzy. This was the Wings' first Cup since 1943.

As NHL president Clarence Campbell handed the Cup over to Wings captain Sid Abel, Howe appeared on the ice to celebrate with his teammates. The roof nearly came off the stadium as the crowd cheered him almost louder than the Stanley Cup victory. "I'll never forget the night he came back, more so than the night he got hurt," Abel remembered. "The night we won it, he got a standing ovation. We were all thrilled." After a stint in the hospital and months of hard rehabilitation, Howe returned the following season and played in all 70 games, scoring 43 goals and 43 assists to win the Art Ross Trophy.

The Production Line

Gordie Howe was the right wing on one of the most famous lines in hockey history—the Production Line—with Ted Lindsay on the left wing and Sid Abel at center. Tommy Ivan had replaced Jack Adams as coach in 1947, and he instantly put Howe and Lindsay around the veteran Abel. Lindsay won the scoring title in 1950, and for the only time in hockey history, the three members of one line finished 1–2–3 in the scoring race. Lindsay had 23 points and 55 assists for 78 points, Abel had 34 goals and 35 assists for 69 points, and Howe had 35 goals and 33 assists for 68 points. Maurice "The Rocket" Richard of Montreal was fourth, with 65 points.

Who Is Billy Taylor?

Not many Detroit Red Wings fans know of Billy Taylor, and with the exception of one game, there would be no reason to remember the center who played only one season for Detroit (1946–47). On March 16, 1947, Taylor recorded seven assists in one game, against the Chicago Blackhawks. It is an NHL record that has been tied but not broken through the 2009–10 season.

The Origin of the Octopus

During the early 1950s, the Red Wings were one of the best teams in hockey. With players like Red Kelly, Terry Sawchuk, Ted Lindsay, Alex Delvecchio and the legendary Gordie Howe, the Wings could always be counted on to give their original five rivals a tough time on the ice. But in the 1952 play-offs, no team could match Detroit's finest.

As there were only six teams in the NHL from 1942 to 1967, it was possible to make a direct line to the Stanley Cup in two series or eight straight games. After polishing off the Toronto Maples Leafs in the opening round in four straight games (two via shutout), the Red Wings went up against the Montreal Canadiens in the final. The games were close, but the Red Wings were the better team and, after three games, Detroit was just one win away from a clean sweep to the Cup.

Brothers Pete and Jerry Cusimano were diehard Red Wings fans and felt that the team's run to the Cup in eight straight games needed something to symbolize the record feat. "My dad was in the fish and poultry business," Pete said. "Anyway, before the eighth game in '52, my brother suggested, 'Why don't we throw an octopus on the ice for good luck? It's got eight legs and that might be a good omen for eight straight wins.'"

On April 15, 1952, the Cusimano brothers carried a half-boiled, slimy octopus into Olympia Stadium, and as the teams held their warm-up skate, Pete grabbed the slippery creature out of his bag and launched the dead cephalopod onto the ice. People in the arena hardly knew what to make of the sea creature's sudden appearance on the ice, but when Detroit went on to win the game and the Stanley Cup in a record eight consecutive games, the story of the octopus got picked up in the papers and a playoff tradition was born.

The Cusimano brothers continued their tradition for the next 15 years, and every time the Red Wings made it into the playoffs, there would be a slimy, wet, eight-legged creature from the deep waiting to greet the home team. Since then, the octopus has become the unofficial mascot of the Detroit Red Wings. Before the start of every home playoff game, a large purple octopus named Al is hung from the rafters of Joe Louis Arena.

The tradition of launching the deceased sea creatures onto the ice became so popular with fans that during one game of the 1995 playoffs, 36 octopi were thrown onto the ice, including one rather large specimen that looked like a creature from *20,000 Leagues Under the Sea*. It has become such an accepted part of Detroit's advancement into the playoffs that fans even developed a code of etiquette and a technique for throwing the octopi onto the ice.

Goodbye, Octopi

To remove these octopi from the ice, the Red Wings turned to Al Sobotka, the head ice manager of Joe Louis Arena. Not satisfied with simply scooping up the sea creatures and placing them in the garbage, Sobotka began twirling the octopi to get the crowd into the game. Fans seemed to love the extra show, but soon NHL director of hockey operations Colin Campbell sent out a memo to Sobotka to stop twirling the octopi because bits of matter could land on the ice, therefore delaying the game. Sobotka's swing had become popular with Wings fans, and once the media got wind of the ban, the Detroit press began to call the prohibition "Octopus-gate." At the beginning of the 2008 playoffs, the NHL relented to public pressure and allowed Sobotka to continue his octopus twirl, but he had to do it just off the ice at the Zamboni entrance.

Copycat

The Red Wings' tradition of throwing dead creatures onto the ice initiated a few other traditions across the league. During the 1995 Stanley Cup playoffs between the New Jersey Devils and the Boston Bruins, an eager Bruins fan threw a lobster onto the ice of Boston Gardens in the hope of imparting some luck to his beloved hockey team. The flinging of seafood continued into the Stanley Cup finals that year when the Devils faced off against the Red Wings. Hoping to combat the luck the Red Wings seemed to take from the octopus, a Devils fan tossed a fish onto the ice after the Devils scored. The Devils won the game, but luckily the tradition of flinging smelly fish did not catch on.

Edmonton Oilers fans took the throwing of food-stuffs to the realm of the ridiculous when they met the Red Wings in the 2006 playoffs. Hoping to start a lucky tradition of their own and, seeing as how the province of Alberta is known for its beef, fans began chucking fresh steaks onto the ice before games. Security put a stop to the steak tossing, arresting anyone who threw a piece of beef.

The tradition of tossing seafood went a little too far during the 2007 playoffs between the San Jose Sharks and the Red Wings, when a crazy Sharks fan threw a four-foot leopard shark onto the ice at HP Pavilion. The fan, Ken Conroy, purchased the shark for $100, then secured the frozen beast to his back with Velcro straps and covered it with a large overcoat. He somehow managed to get past security and was able to toss the fish onto the ice. Luckily, that tradition didn't catch on, either.

Stupid Trades

Norris Trophy–winning defenseman Red Kelly was one of the key ingredients to the success of the Detroit Red Wings in the 1950s and helped the team to four Stanley Cups during his tenure on the Detroit blue line. He was still a young player with years of good hockey ahead of him in 1959 when he broke his ankle in midseason. Despite the pain radiating throughout his body, Kelly managed to play the remainder of the season while keeping the injury a secret.

It was midway through the following season when a reporter asked Kelly why he had been subpar the previous year. Kelly replied, "Don't know. Might have been the ankle." When Red Wings general manager Jack Adams heard that the secret had been spilled, he was furious and immediately traded Kelly to the Toronto Maple Leafs for defenseman Marc Reaume. That he would trade a player who had disobeyed one of his orders was not much of a surprise to those who knew of Adams' legendary temper, but to trade a quality player like Kelly for an unknown defenseman was viewed as hasty. The trade proved a boon for the Maple Leafs, who went on to win four Stanley Cups with Kelly in their lineup, while the Wings did not win another Cup until 1997. Marc Reaume played in only 47 games with the Red Wings.

Some 20 years later, the Red Wings made yet another poor trade under adverse conditions. The Red Wings were in the middle of their "Dead Wings" era, and *Sports Illustrated* had written an article about the team entitled, "Poor, Broken Wings." Detroit had the number two overall selection in the 1971 NHL draft and picked Marcel Dionne, a high-scoring star from the Ontario

Hockey League. Dionne spent four seasons in Detroit, and the Red Wings failed to make the play-offs in any of those seasons. When Dionne's contract expired at the end of the 1974–75 season, he requested a trade. Detroit traded him and Bart Crashley to the Los Angeles Kings for Terry Harper, Don Maloney and a second-round draft pick. Dionne, who scored 139 goals with 227 assists for Detroit in four seasons, finished his career with 731 goals and 1040 assists.

Gordie's All-Star Return

Joe Louis Arena had been the home of the Red Wings for less than two months when the NHL All-Star Game visited Detroit on February 5, 1980. Red Wings fans were in for a special treat—Gordie Howe, who had retired as a member of the Red Wings in 1971, was making his return to Detroit as an All-Star player from the Hartford Whalers. A crowd of 21,002 gave Mr. Hockey a four-minute standing ovation that likely would have lasted longer, except that announcer John Bell interceded to introduce the singers for the national anthem.

Howe was on the Wales Conference team, which was coached by future Red Wings coach Scotty Bowman. Howe had 11 goals at the All-Star break and some suggested that he wasn't worthy of playing in the All-Star Game. Bowman disagreed. "I said if Gordie didn't play, I wouldn't coach," Bowman said. "It was a natural for him to play that game in Detroit. I didn't care what anybody thought. I knew he could still play, and it turned out perfect." Although Howe did not score in the All-Star Game, he did draw an assist on the final goal of the game as the Wales Conference won 6–3.

The Russian Five

In 1995, Red Wings coach Scotty Bowman shuffled his lineup and put five Russian players on the ice at the same time for the first time in NHL history. Slava Kozlov, Igor Larionov and Sergie Fedorov were the forwards, paired with defensemen Vladimir Konstantinov and Slava Fetisov. The Red Wings won 3–0 as Kozlov and Larionov each scored a goal and Fedorov had two assists.

The Russian Five would play a big role in the Red Wings' success in the coming years. Fedorov, who had won the Hart Trophy as the league MVP in 1994–95, scored all five goals for the Red Wings in a 5–4 victory against the Washington Capitals on December 26, 1996. Konstantiov drew four assists in the game, and the Russian Five finished with eight of the team's nine points.

"They do two things really well," Washington coach Jim Schoenfeld told *The Associated Press* of the Russians. "The puck is always in motion and all five players are always in motion."

Stanley Cup Drought Ends

When the Detroit Red Wings won their first two Stanley Cups back to back in 1936 and 1937, fans got used to the idea of their team being champions. The boys in red would win another five cups, with the final one coming in 1955 over the Montreal Canadiens. But for the next few decades, the Detroit Red Wings couldn't seem to string together the required number of wins in the play-offs to take the Cup. From 1956 until 1996, the Red Wings made it into the finals a total of six times and failed to convert.

Scotty Bowman, the coach with the most wins in the history of the NHL, took over the Red Wings in 1993, and Detroit finished the 1994–95 strike-shortened season with the best record in the league. Bowman led his squad to the Stanley Cup finals for the first time since 1966, this time against the New Jersey Devils, but they ended up losing the series in four straight games.

The Wings returned more determined than ever for the 1995–96 regular season, and they won an incredible 62 games, lost 13 and tied 7 for a total of 131 points. Their season ranks as second best in league history, and they moved into the conference finals against the Colorado Avalanche, but they could not solve goalie Patrick Roy and his team. The Wings were out of the race yet again.

The following season was not as successful for the Wings, but they managed to reach the conference finals. It would be the Red Wings against the defending Stanley Cup champions, the Colorado Avalanche.

The Wings were out for more than just a simple victory over the Avalanche—they wanted complete revenge. It was just one year ago, around the exact same time, that professional on-ice pest Claude Lemieux of the Avalanche delivered a vicious check from behind on Kris Draper, sending him crashing into the boards face first. The fall fractured Draper's nose, broke his jaw and cheekbone and gave him a severe concussion. The worst part for many of the Detroit players was that Lemieux never apologized or showed any remorse for the hit that could have ended Draper's career. Earlier in the season, the two teams had met and settled their accounts in an all-out, old-school brawl involving all the players on the ice and two goalies.

Tensions ran high, and the Red Wings eventually got retribution in a 4–2 series win over Colorado. The Wings certainly enjoyed the sweet taste of revenge, but they had not won the Cup just yet and still had to get past a very difficult Philadelphia Flyers squad before they could celebrate their first Stanley Cup victory since 1955.

Ever since the 1970s Broad Street Bullies edition of the Philadelphia Flyers, the team had maintained an image as a tough team to play. The 1997 playoff version of the Flyers was no different from past incarnations, with physically imposing players like "The Big E" Eric Lindros, John LeClair and Rod Brind'Amour. Despite all the heavy weaponry, the Flyers were still no match for the Red Wings, who swept past them in four straight games on the way to the franchise's first Stanley Cup in 42 years.

Tragedy After Triumph

The Red Wings won the Stanley Cup on June 7, 1997, with a 2–1 victory over the Flyers at Joe Louis Arena. Darren McCarty had scored the winning goal on a Saturday night, and Detroit erupted into a peaceful, weeklong party to celebrate its well-earned trophy. But the celebrations were cut short the following Friday—Friday the 13th—when a limousine carrying Red Wings defenseman Vladimir Konstantinov, forward Slava Fetisov and team masseur Sergei Mnatsakanov lost control and slammed into a tree on Woodward Avenue in Birmingham. Fetisov emerged from the wreck with minor cuts and bruises, but Konstantinov suffered far more serious injuries that ended his career and left him physically handicapped and confined to a wheelchair for the remainder of his life. Mnatsakanov suffered severe head injuries and spent time in a coma.

Richard Gnida, the driver of the limousine, did not have a valid driver's license and apparently had fallen asleep.

An Emotional Stanley Cup

Often it is said that a team does not have the motivation necessary to repeat after winning a championship, but that was not the case with the

1997–98 Detroit Red Wings. Although Fetisov was able to return to the ice, Konstantinov was not, and Mnatsakanov was having a difficult recovery and was not with the team. The Red Wings wanted to win the title for Konstantinov, and that's just what they did.

The Red Wings finished second in the Central Division behind Dallas but still had the third-most points in the league. Detroit beat Phoenix in six games to move on to the second round of the play-offs, where they overcame the St. Louis Blues in six games to earn a spot in the Western Conference finals. Their opponent was the Central Division champion Dallas Stars, and for the third series in a row, the Red Wings won in six games, setting the stage for a meeting with the Washington Capitals in the Stanley Cup finals. Detroit took the first four games to win a second consecutive Stanley Cup and the ninth in franchise history. Steve Yzerman won the Conn Smythe Trophy and, as captain, was the first to receive the Stanley Cup. After hoisting the Cup, Yzerman placed it in the lap of Konstantinov, who had been wheeled onto the ice for his moment with his former teammates. It was one of the most emotional moments in the history of the Stanley Cup.

Hang 10

Throughout the first decade of the 21st century, the Red Wings continued to be a force in the NHL. They extended their streak of making the playoffs to

19 consecutive years and made three appearances in the Stanley Cup finals. By most accounts, the one weakness on the team was the lack of a solid, veteran goaltender, so prior to the 2001–02 season, the Red Wings went out and signed one of the best—Dominik Hasek, who had led the Czech national team to the gold medal in the 1998 Olympic Games.

Detroit piled up 116 points in the 2001–02 season. In the first round of the playoffs, the Vancouver Canucks threw a scare into the Red Wings by winning the first two games at Joe Louis Arena, but Detroit answered with four consecutive victories to advance to the second round, where they faced the St. Louis Blues. Things went considerably smoother this time as Detroit eliminated St. Louis in five games, earning a spot in the conference finals against fierce rival Colorado and goalie Patrick Roy.

Detroit and Colorado had a rabid rivalry since the mid-1990s, and Roy was one of the main villains ever since the famous 1996 regular-season game when he went toe to toe with then–Red Wings goalie Mike Vernon at center ice. The first six games were tight, as there were three overtime games (Colorado won two of them), and the series was tied. In Game 7, Roy was peppered by the Red Wings, who defeated Colorado 7–0 to earn a spot in the Stanley Cup finals against Carolina.

Carolina stunned Detroit in Game 1 by winning 3–2 in overtime, but the Red Wings and Hasek allowed just four goals over the next four games and won the Stanley Cup in five games for the 10th Stanley Cup championship in franchise history. Detroit became the first team in NHL history to win the Stanley Cup after losing its first two games at home. Defenseman Nicklas Lidstrom was the winner of the Conn Smythe Trophy as the most valuable player in the playoffs.

The 2001–02 team is considered one of the most talented teams in the history of the NHL. The team had as many as nine current or future Hall of Famers, not counting legendary coach Scotty Bowman: Steve Yzerman, Brendan Shanahan, Luc Robitaille, Brett Hull, Igor Larionov, Sergei Fedorov, Chris Chelios, Nicklas Lidstrom and Dominik Hasek. Incidentally, after the Red Wings won the Stanley Cup, captain Steve Yzerman lifted the Cup and handed it to Bowman, who stunned everyone when he put on a pair of skates to take a short trip around the ice while holding the Stanley Cup. Bowman retired after the game.

A New-look Championship

With the retirement of coach Scotty Bowman after the 2001–02 season, and the retirement of longtime captain Steve Yzerman after the 2005–06 season, the Red Wings had a different look late in the decade. Dave Lewis succeeded Bowman as coach but lasted just two seasons as he did not have enough playoff success, losing in the first round once and in the second round another time. Lewis was replaced by Mike Babcock, who had coached the Anaheim Mighty Ducks to the Stanley Cup finals in the 2002–03 season. Detroit finished first in their division in each of Babcock's first four seasons, with defenseman Nicklas Lidstrom as Yzerman's successor in the position of team captain. The change worked wonders, as Detroit went on to win the Stanley Cup with a 3–2 victory against the Pittsburgh Penguins in Game 6 at Joe Louis Arena in 2008.

Chapter Four

"DEEEEE-troit Basket-BALL"

From Olympia Stadium to Cobo Arena, from Cobo to the Silverdome in Pontiac, and finally, from the Silverdome to The Palace of Auburn Hills, Detroit basketball fans have followed their Pistons faithfully for more than 50 years. For most of the early years, frustration was the most common emotion felt by fans, but in the past 20 or so years, the Pistons have delivered three NBA championships and offered Detroit basketball fans a contending team more often than not.

Local radio personality John Mason took over as the public address announcer at The Palace in 2001—about the same time the team returned to being a contender. Mason's colorful introductions were a hit with the fans, and during timeouts he would yell to the crowd, "Deeeee-troit basket-BALL," and the chant caught on in a big way. It became the signature of the Detroit teams during the latter part of the first decade of the 21st century.

The Fort Wayne Pistons

It would seem normal to think that the Detroit Pistons got their nickname because Detroit is the automobile capital of the world, but that's not the case. The Pistons originated in Fort Wayne, Indiana, in 1941 when businessman Fred Zollner bought the team and called it the Fort Wayne Zollner Pistons. Zollner ran a foundry that manufactured pistons for engines. The team played in the National Basketball League and moved to the competing Basketball Association of America in 1948. Eventually, the NBL merged with the BAA to form the National Basketball Association, which is known today as the NBA. After the 1957 season, Zollner moved the team to Detroit because he felt Fort Wayne was not large enough to support an NBA team, and the name Pistons was a natural for a team from Detroit.

The Early Years

The Pistons' first home in Detroit was Olympia Stadium, the home of the Detroit Red Wings, and they played their first two games there. The Pistons played their first game in Detroit on October 23, 1957, and lost to the Boston Celtics 105–94 before a crowd of nearly 11,000.

Three days later, the Pistons were home against the Philadelphia Warriors, but lost again 112–100. Finally, on October 30, the Detroit team finally won a game—a 114–96 victory over the Minneapolis Lakers on the road.

After 25 games, the Pistons were 9–16, and coach Charley Eckman, who came with the team from Fort Wayne, was fired and replaced by Red Rocha. They finished the season with a 33–39 record, and it was good enough for second place in the Western Conference and a spot in the NBA playoffs. Detroit reached the conference finals, but they were eliminated by the St. Louis Hawks in five games.

George Yardley was Detroit's first professional basketball star, leading the league in scoring with 27.8 points per game. Rocha coached the team until December 27, 1959, when he was let go after a five-game losing streak. Despite a 28–44 record, the Pistons returned to the NBA playoffs in 1959, their second season in Detroit, but lost to the Minneapolis Lakers in a three-game series.

A Home in Downtown Detroit

It seemed nothing would change for the Pistons in Detroit. They would finish with a sub-.500 record, make the playoffs and lose in the first round. But they landed a new home for the 1961–62 season—Cobo Arena in downtown Detroit. Their first game at Cobo took place on October 25, 1961, when the Pistons lost to the Boston Celtics 120–116. The Pistons' first win in their new stadium came on November 1, 1961, when they beat the New York Knicks 111–95. However, playing at Cobo Arena did little to change what was happening on the court. The Pistons finished with yet another sub-.500 record (37–43) and lost to the Los Angeles Lakers in the Western Conference finals.

The Youngest Player-coach

Things actually got worse for the Pistons after the move to Cobo, and the team made a drastic move on November 9, 1964, when they hired 6-foot-6, 24-year-old forward Dave DeBusschere to serve as player-coach. Growing up in Detroit, DeBusschere had been a star at the University of Detroit, and the Pistons chose him fourth overall in the 1962 NBA draft. He had also been a star baseball pitcher in college, and the Chicago White Sox had offered him a $75,000 signing bonus. He played professional baseball for four years and made it to the big leagues with the White Sox in 1963, when he went 3–4 with a 3.09 ERA.

Meanwhile, DeBusschere's first years with the Pistons did not go so well. He averaged 12.7 points per game in his first season and was named to the NBA All-Rookie team, but he broke his arm in his second season and played just 15 games. At that point, DeBusschere was offered the position of player-coach, possibly to force his hand and make him quit baseball and focus entirely on basketball. He spent one more season in professional baseball and actually declined a call-up to the majors by the White Sox in 1965. The Pistons' strategy had worked.

With baseball out of the picture, the Pistons relieved DeBusschere of his coaching duties after the 1966–67 season, and he finished with a 79–143 record as a coach. "It was a relief to give up coaching," he later told *Newsday*. "I realize now there were things I wasn't mature enough to handle. As soon as I was back on my own again, I had my best season. I was scoring better, rebounding better, defending better and doing everything else better."

Still, DeBusschere's solid play was not helping the Pistons win more games, so late in 1968, Detroit traded him to the New York Knicks for center Walt Bellamy and guard Howard Komives. It turned out to be a great deal for the Knicks as DeBusschere helped the team win two NBA titles, and he ended up in the Basketball Hall of Fame.

Losing a Coin Flip…and Winning

The Pistons finished last in the Western Conference in the 1965–66 season, and the New York Knicks were last in the Eastern Conference. For the first time, the two last-place teams would get the first two picks in the NBA draft, but a coin flip would be used to determine which team would get the first pick. Cazzie Russell, the all-American from the University of Michigan, had been the player of the year in college and was the consensus choice to be the first player taken in the draft. Russell, who had a huge following in Michigan, would be a huge spark for the Pistons in terms of winning games and fans, so there was considerable frustration when the Knicks won the coin toss and chose Russell with the number-one pick. The dejected Pistons were left with the second pick and chose guard Dave Bing of Syracuse. Bing quickly became Detroit's first true basketball star and was named the NBA Rookie of the Year.

Bing played in seven NBA All-Star games and was the MVP of the game in 1976. He played nine seasons in Detroit but became frustrated with the team's lack of success. He also wanted a chance to play closer to his home in Washington, DC, so prior to the 1975–76 season, the Pistons traded Bing and a first-round pick to the Washington Bullets for guard Kevin Porter. But Bing's best days were behind him, and he retired after the 1977–78 season.

After Bing concluded his playing days, he returned to Detroit to work at Paragon Steel. It turned out to be a great move, as Bing found a home in the steel business, and in 1980, he opened Bing Steel in Detroit. He became one of the most success-ful businessmen in the city, and in 2009, he was elected the 70th mayor of Detroit. It makes one wonder what would have happened had Detroit won that coin toss back in 1966.

The Dobber

After 13 consecutive losing seasons in Detroit, the Pistons were looking for a star player to pair with young guard Dave Bing. They had the first pick in the 1970 NBA draft and chose Bob Lanier, a 6-foot-11 center out of St. Bonaventure. It was a great pick. Lanier spent more than nine seasons in Detroit, averaging 22.7 points per game and grabbing more than 8000 rebounds, though he suffered several nagging injuries over the years. Shoulder, back and elbow problems dogged him, and he had issues with his knees.

Nicknamed "The Dobber," a way of combining his name, Bob, with "Big Dipper," Wilt Chamberlain's nickname, Lanier finally tired of losing in Detroit and requested a trade early in the 1979–80 season. He was dealt to the Milwaukee Bucks for Kent Benson and a first-round draft pick. The Bucks were more successful than the Pistons had been, but they failed to win a championship. Lanier was inducted into the Basketball Hall of Fame, but never realized his dream of winning an NBA title.

When Lanier retired in 1984, he said he did so only because the Bucks had found a player in Alton Lister who could fill his shoes. Lister, like Lanier, wore an incredible size 22 shoe.

Goodbye Cobo, Hello Pontiac

The Pistons said goodbye to Cobo Arena and downtown Detroit on April 9, 1978, as 3482 fans showed up for the final game at Cobo. It was an entertaining game as the Pistons beat Denver 139–137 despite 73 points by Nuggets star David Thompson, who was trying to win the NBA scoring title. His big effort meant that Detroit native

George Gervin had to score at least 58 points that night for San Antonio to edge Thompson for the scoring title, and Gervin responded with 66 points on that final day of the season.

The Pistons moved to the huge Silverdome in Pontiac, the domed home of the Detroit Lions of the NFL. Detroit lost its first game at the Silverdome to New Jersey 107–105 on October 13, 1978, and their first win at the Silverdome came 12 days later in a 110–105 victory over Cleveland. The Pistons spent 10 seasons at the Silverdome, setting attendance records along the way. More than one million people saw Pistons games at the Silverdome in the 1987–88 season, the final one in Pontiac. A record crowd of 61,983 attended the game against the Boston Celtics on January 29, 1988.

Dickie V.

Long before Dick Vitale was a colorful college basketball announcer, he was a basketball coach at the University of Detroit. Vitale was successful with the Titans, helping them to a 78–30 record, including a 21-game winning streak in 1977. The Pistons took notice and hired him as coach prior to the 1978–79 season, but it just didn't work out. The Pistons were 30–52 in their first season under Vitale, and just 12 games into the following season, the Pistons fired him and he took a job at a fledgling sports network called ESPN. As Dickie V. would say, "The rest is history, baby."

Zeke

Just like in the 1966 NBA draft, the Pistons had the number two overall selection in the 1981 NBA draft. And, like in 1966 when the Pistons drafted a future Hall of Famer in Dave Bing, the Pistons hit the jackpot again with the selection of Isiah Thomas of Indiana. Thomas, a 6-foot-tall point guard, is known as one of the best small men in the history of the NBA, and he became a leader in Detroit. The Pistons were coming off a 21–61 record in the 1980–81 season, and Thomas immediately made the team better in his rookie season. Detroit improved by 18 wins as Thomas averaged 17 points and 7.8 assists as a rookie. He also made the first of 12 consecutive trips to the NBA All-Star Game.

Thomas had led Indiana to the NCAA championship as a sophomore in 1981, and he was more concerned with winning championships than he was putting up gaudy numbers. Nothing was more important to Thomas, known as "Zeke," than winning. It was going to be quite a decade.

Two Teams, 370 Points

It was nothing more than a typical, early-season game in Denver between two teams not expected to contend for the NBA championship. It turned out to be the highest-scoring game in league history. On December 13, 1983, the Pistons defeated Denver 186–184 in triple overtime, setting the league record with 370 combined points. Part of the reason was the three overtime periods, and another part of the reason was Nuggets coach Doug Moe, who played an up-tempo, offensive-minded style of basketball. Six Pistons scored in double-figures: Isiah Thomas (47), John Long (41), Kelly Tripucka (35), Terry Tyler (18), Bill Laimbeer (17) and Vinnie Johnson (12). Kiki Vandeweghe of Denver scored a game-high 51 points.

"At that time, if you go to Denver, you know you're going to be in for a scoring match," Pistons forward Kelly Tripucka said on nba.com. "They didn't run a lot of plays, they just kept running. We knew we had to play a certain way with them."

Daddy Rich

It was a slow-but-sure process as the Pistons put together a championship team. Isiah Thomas was the first piece, quickly followed by the acquisition of Bill Laimbeer from Cleveland on February 16, 1982. But perhaps the most important of all was the hiring of Chuck Daly as coach prior to the 1983–84 season. Daly had been a successful college coach at Penn, but he endured a miserable 9–32 record with the 1981–82 Cleveland Cavaliers. The Pistons ignored that lack of success and hired him anyway, and they couldn't have made a better choice. He was a players' coach but could be stern and get his message across when he wanted. The Pistons grew up under Daly, whom forward John Salley called "Daddy Rich" because of Daly's impeccable style of dressing.

In Daly's first season, the Pistons finished 49–33 and in second place in the Central Division. They also ended a seven-year playoff drought, but they lost an epic five-game series to the New York Knicks in the first round of the playoffs. In a classic Game 5, the Pistons succumbed to the Knicks 127–123 in overtime as Thomas and New York's Bernard King each gave brilliant performances. Thomas scored 16 points in the final 94 seconds of regulation time to force overtime. King finished with 44 points for the Knicks.

The Pistons had their court leader in Thomas, and with the hiring of Daly, they found their teacher and father figure. And they were winning.

The Bad Boys

They had their coach. They had their floor leader. And, in time, they earned an identity— that of a rough-and-tough basketball team that played with a no-holds-barred attitude. If you drive in the lane, expect to be hit and hit hard. Defense was the name of the game, and it wasn't a soft defense, either. The Pistons became known as the "Bad Boys," hated in NBA arenas around the nation, and the biggest villains were Laimbeer and Rick Mahorn, two very physical players. In many other NBA cities, the word "physical" might be replaced with the word "dirty." That didn't bother the Pistons, and, in fact, they embraced it. They even decided to practice in black jerseys with the skull and crossbones of the Oakland Raiders—the perennial Bad Boys of the National Football League. In fact, Al Davis, owner of the Raiders, sent the jerseys to the Pistons. All that was left to do was learn to win.

The Pistons went up against the more experienced Boston Celtics in the 1987 NBA Eastern Conference finals. The series was tied 2–2 prior to Game 5, the last game of the series to be played in Boston. The Pistons were on the verge of a victory when Larry Bird stole an inbounds pass by Isiah Thomas and fed it to Dennis Johnson for a game-winning layup. The Pistons never recovered, and the Celtics went on to win the series. But the Pistons didn't forget. The following season, it was the Pistons and Celtics again in the conference finals, and this time, the Pistons got their revenge by winning in six games to earn a spot in the NBA finals for the first time.

Just like the previous year, another heartbreaking loss was in store for the Pistons. They led the best-of-seven series three games to two when they returned to Los Angeles, and the Pistons were in a position to win the championship when Thomas suffered a sprained ankle. He put on one of the most memorable performances in NBA finals history by hobbling his way to 25 points in the third quarter, but the Lakers escaped with a 103–102 victory. With Thomas at less-than-full strength, the Pistons fell short in Game 7, 108–105, and once again they were left to deal with a tough loss over the offseason.

Another New Home

After 10 seasons at the Silverdome in Pontiac, the Pistons moved another few miles to the north into a new, state-of-the-art complex called The Palace of Auburn Hills. The last game at the Silverdome had been Game 5 of the 1988 NBA finals and, even though the Palace had less seating capacity than the Silverdome, there was a lot of excitement about the move. The first 245 games at the Palace sold out, partly because of the success of the team and partly because of the sharp new facility.

NBA Champions

There was one piece remaining to be added to the championship puzzle, and on February 15, 1989, the Pistons traded Adrian Dantley, their leading scorer, and a future number-one draft pick to the Dallas Mavericks for Mark Aguirre. Dantley had clashed with coach Chuck Daly. "There was tension between Daly and Dantley; the coach felt he was holding the ball too long, leaving the offense scrambling for last-second shots. The Pistons also felt A.D. wasn't getting to the foul line enough," Steve Addy of the *Oakland Press* wrote in his book, *Four Decades of Motor City Memories*. With Aguirre in the lineup, the Pistons lost their first two games and three of the first six before going on a nine-game winning streak, and they won 30 of their last 34 regular-season games. They were ready for the playoffs.

The Boston Celtics, who had stumbled a bit in the 1988–89 season, were the opponents in the first round, but the Pistons dispatched them in three games. The streak continued as Detroit swept Milwaukee in four games in the second round to move to the conference finals against the upstart Chicago Bulls and their superstar player, Michael Jordan. The Bulls threw a scare into the Pistons by winning two of the first three games, but Detroit reeled off three consecutive victories to win the conference title and earn a rematch in the NBA finals with the Los Angeles Lakers.

This time, Isiah Thomas was healthy. The Pistons won the first two games at home, and as the series moved to Los Angeles, it was the Lakers who had an injured star as former Michigan State star Magic Johnson was hobbled. The Pistons never let up and won two more games at the Forum in Los Angeles to complete the sweep and win their first NBA championship.

MVP of the NBA Finals

While Isiah Thomas was the face of the Pistons, it was another guard, Joe Dumars, who was team's heart. An unheralded player when he was drafted out of McNeese State in 1985, Dumars scrapped his high-scoring style to become more defensive-minded to fit in better with the Pistons' needs. He also was the center of the famous "Jordan Rules," the strategy designed to limit Bulls superstar

Michael Jordan. Dumars was supposed to keep Jordan from driving to his right when he was at the top of the key and not let him go to the middle when he was on the wing. This strategy helped the Pistons defeat the Bulls in the postseason three years in a row.

In fact, Dumars was maybe the only Pistons player who didn't fit the Bad Boys image. He was the consummate nice guy, a classy professional who had earned the respect of everyone in the league. He also hadn't forgotten how to score, and he showed it in the 1989 NBA finals. Dumars averaged 27.3 points per game in the four-game sweep of the Lakers and was named the MVP of the NBA finals. He was finally escaping the shadow of Isiah Thomas.

0.07

As the Pistons drove to another NBA championship, they encountered very little resistance. They finished the regular season 59–23 and swept the Indiana Pacers, the New York Knicks and the Chicago Bulls to set up a return to the NBA finals. Instead of the Los Angeles Lakers, it was the Portland TrailBlazers who awaited the Pistons.

Detroit put on a sloppy performance in Game 1 of the finals. They escaped with a 105–99 victory, but Portland evened the series in Game 2 with a 106–105 win. With the finals shifting to Portland for the next three games, there was some doubt in Detroit, but the Pistons swept the next three games to repeat as NBA champions. In the deciding Game 5, the score was 90–90 when Thomas passed the ball to Vinnie Johnson, who had earned the nickname "Microwave" because he could heat up so quickly. Johnson, an excellent shooter, had been hot, and he hit the game-winning and championship-winning jumper with just 0.07 seconds left on the clock. The game, and the season, was over, and Detroit cele-brated another championship.

This time, Thomas was named the MVP of the NBA finals and not Dumars. But Dumars had much more on his mind. His father had died of congestive heart failure on June 10, 1990, the same day as Game 3 of the NBA finals, and Dumars had elected to stay with his team until the end of the series. He wasn't able to totally celebrate the Pistons' NBA championship because he had to fly home for his father's funeral at the conclusion of the series.

The Worm

Before Dennis Rodman became the multicolored-hair wacko and rebounding machine of the NBA, he was a little-known reserve known as "The Worm" on the Pistons' championship teams. He spent his first seven seasons in the NBA with Detroit and was comfortable playing under coach Chuck Daly, who had a calming effect on him. But as the Bad Boys team was breaking up and started losing more often, Rodman became a disgruntled, con-fused and misunderstood young man. Twice he was named the NBA Defensive Player of the Year while a member of the Pistons, and he cried openly upon receiving the awards.

Rodman's days in Detroit nearly reached a tragic end in May 1993, when police found him asleep in his car one night in the Palace parking lot with a loaded rifle. Rodman wrote of that experience in his autobiography, *As Bad as I Want to Be*: "I decided that instead (of killing myself) I was gonna kill the impostor that was leading Dennis Rodman to a place he didn't want to go…. So I just said, 'I'm going to live my life the way I want to live it and be happy doing it.' At that moment, I tamed [sic] my whole life around. I killed the person I didn't want to be."

A few months later, Rodman requested a trade, and he was dealt to the San Antonio Spurs. He eventually played with the Bulls, where he won three more championship rings.

The Bust of the Draft

After his playing days with the Pistons, Joe Dumars remained with the organization as vice-president of player personnel and president of basketball operations. So Dumars was faced with a huge decision in 2003 when the Pistons had the number-two pick in a talent-laden NBA draft. Detroit chose forward Darko Milicic from Serbia—a highly touted player—but Milicic remained a controversial pick in Detroit because he was not an American player. He spent two and a half seasons with the Pistons before he was traded to Orlando with Carlos Arroyo for Kelvin Cato and a draft pick that turned out to be Rodney Stuckey. Through six seasons in the NBA, Milicic was nothing more than a journeyman player, and it was uncertain whether he would remain in America or return to Europe to play basketball.

It wasn't bad enough that Milicic was a bust. The real pain came from the all-star players who were chosen after Milicic: Carmelo Anthony by Denver at number three, Chris Bosh by Toronto at number four, Dwyane Wade by Miami at number five and Chris Kaman by the Los Angeles Clippers at number six.

Champions Again

The post–Bad Boy days were rough for Pistons fans starting in the 1992–93 season. The team made the playoffs just four times in the next nine seasons and lost in the first round every time. But the 2001–02 season signaled a turnaround as they improved and took first place in the Central Division. In fact, from 2001–02 through 2007–08, the Pistons won the Central Division every year but one and made six consecutive appearances in the Eastern Conference finals. The highlight came in the 2003–04 season when the Pistons shocked the world and won the NBA title, beating Kobe Bryant, Shaquille O'Neal and the Los Angeles Lakers in five games in the finals.

Larry Brown, a much-traveled coach, replaced Rick Carlisle prior to the 2003–04 season. The team got off to a 32–16 start under their new coach before losing six consecutive games prior to the All-Star break. The NBA championship seemed like a long shot when the playoffs started, and at times the Pistons were seemingly on the verge of losing it all. However, Detroit was able to advance to the conference finals, where they met up with the Indiana Pacers.

Carlisle, who had coached the Pistons the previous two seasons, was now the Indiana coach, and there was some tension in the series. Detroit won in six hard-fought games to earn a spot in the finals against the Lakers, who were heavy favorites. Detroit shocked the Lakers and the rest of the basketball fans by winning Game 1 and nearly taking Game 2. However, Bryant hit a dramatic three-point shot with 2.1 seconds left to force overtime, and Los Angeles squared the series at 1–1 with a 99–91 victory.

The series returned to The Palace, where Detroit ran off three consecutive victories to win their third NBA title in franchise history. Chauncey Billups, who had found a home in Detroit after playing for Boston, Toronto, Denver and Minnesota, was named the MVP of the NBA finals. Detroit returned to the finals the following season and nearly won another championship but lost to the San Antonio Spurs 81–74 in Game 7 in San Antonio.

The Pistons lost in the conference finals in each of the next three seasons, and they traded Billups to Denver during the 2008–09 season, which seemed to take the heart out of the team. Detroit lost in the first round of the playoffs that season, and in 2009–10, the Pistons had their eight-year streak of making the playoffs end with a 27–55 record, their worst since the 1993–94 season.

Malice at The Palace

It was the season after the Pistons' 2004 NBA championship, and the Indiana Pacers were at The Palace in a rematch of the previous season's Eastern Conference finals. There was no love lost between the teams, but nobody could have expected what happened with less than a minute to go on November 19, 2004. A fight broke out on the court, and as some players argued in front of the scorer's table, a Pistons fan named John Green threw cup of soda at Ron Artest of the Pacers. Artest and teammate Stephen Jackson went into the stands to confront the fan, and a brawl began between the players and the fans. A few fans even ran onto the court and took swings at the Pacers. The remaining seconds of the game were called off, and the Pacers had to dodge debris thrown at them as they retreated to their locker room.

It was one of the ugliest encounters between fans and players in sports history. Artest was suspended for the remainder of the season, and an additional nine players were suspended for a total of 146 games. Green, the fan who threw the cup of soda at Artest, and Charles Haddad, another fan, were banned from attending Pistons home games for life.

Women Can Play, Too

It took a few years for Detroit's newest professional basketball team, the Detroit Shock of the Women's National Basketball Association, to establish a winning tradition, but that's exactly what they did. The Shock entered the WNBA as an expansion team in 1998 and experienced some early growing pains, making the playoffs just once in their first five seasons and hitting a franchise-low 9–23 record in 2002.

Legendary women's player Nancy Lieberman was the first coach of the Shock, and her successor, Greg Williams, was fired early in the miserable 2002 season. His replacement was former Pistons star Bill Laimbeer, and the team's turnaround was faster than anyone could have imagined. The Shock went 25–9 in 2003—the best record in franchise history—and went on to win the WNBA championship.

The Shock hovered around .500 the next two seasons and lost in the first round of the playoffs in both seasons. However, from 2006 through 2008, they made the WNBA finals in all three seasons, winning the title in 2006 and 2008 and losing in the finals to Phoenix in five games in 2007. Some of the same stars that helped the 2003 team win the title were back in 2006, but Detroit had a new sharp-shooting star. Veteran guard Katie Smith, acquired from Minnesota during the 2005 season, made a jumper with 14 seconds left in Game 5 of the WNBA finals to help Detroit secure a victory over the Sacramento Monarchs.

Detroit lost to the Phoenix Mercury in Game 5 of the 2007 WNBA finals, but rebounded in 2008 for the third title in franchise history. This time, there was no late drama as Detroit swept San Antonio in three games to win the championship.

Early in the following season, Laimbeer left the team, and Rick Mahorn, one of the Bad Boys from the Pistons' first championship team and Laimbeer's assistant for many years, took over as coach. The Shock went 18–16 and lost in the conference finals to Indiana. Shortly after the conclusion of the season, it was announced that the team was leaving Detroit to relocate to Tulsa.

Chapter Five

College Athletics: A State Divided

If you live in Michigan, it's hard to be a Spartans *and* a Wolverines fan, and if you are, you're in a vast minority. So, to fully understand what each school is all about, you have to consider the source.

The University of Michigan is the big school—the football school with the most victories in NCAA Division I history—and its academic requirements are higher than those of Michigan State. Talk to Michigan fans and you can sense their feeling of superiority. Maybe that's why Michigan State football coach Darryl Rogers referred to Michigan players as "arrogant asses" during a banquet in 1978.

Michigan State is more down to earth—East Lansing has a lower cost of living, the school is easier to get into and the basketball team has become one of the premier programs in the country. Maybe that's why former Michigan tailback Michael Hart had this to say after Michigan State won a football game against the Wolverines: "Sometimes, you get your little brother excited when you're playing—let them get the lead. And then you come back."

The battle lines are drawn.

The Spartans and the Wolverines

Michigan State was originally known as Michigan Agricultural College, and its nickname was "Aggies" for the first quarter of the 20th century. When the school was renamed Michigan State College in 1925, a contest was held to determine a new nickname. The college picked "The Michigan Staters," which George S. Alderton, sports editor of the *Lansing State Journal*, believed was too cumbersome for newspapers. Alderton was able to go through all the entries, and he chose "Spartans" and used it in headlines during the college's 1926 southern baseball trip. Nobody complained, and Spartans became Michigan State's official nickname.

Things aren't quite as clear as to how the University of Michigan's teams became known as the Wolverines, but the name has been in use since 1861. In fact, nobody knows for sure how it came about, but in 1944, legendary football coach Fielding H. Yost wrote in the *Michigan Quarterly* that he believed the nickname was because of Michigan's activity in trading wolverine pelts in Sault Ste. Marie. Yost believed the traders might have referred to the furs as Michigan wolverines, thus the origin of the nickname.

The First Football Games

Michigan's first football game was held on May 30, 1879, against Racine at White Stockings Park in Chicago. Michigan won 1–0. The Wolverines did not play again until November 1, 1879, when they battled Toronto to a 0–0 tie in Detroit. Michigan's first game in Ann Arbor was held May 12, 1883, when the Wolverines played the Detroit Industrial team. The Wolverines won 40–5.

At Michigan Agricultural College, the first official game was played in 1896, though there is a team photo of the 1884 group that never played a game. In their first game, the Aggies defeated Lansing High School 10–0 as George Wells scored all 10 points for MAC. The game was played at Elton Park in Lansing. The Aggies finished 1–2–1 in their first year.

A Rivalry Begins

On October 12, 1898, Michigan hosted Michigan Agricultural College in the first meeting of what would become the fiercest college football rivalry in the state. Michigan, en route to an 11–0 season, defeated the Aggies 39–0 in Ann Arbor. Interestingly, the game was played on a Wednesday afternoon. Four years later, again on a Wednesday afternoon, Michigan pounded the Aggies 119–0 on their way to the national championship.

Counting the 2009 season, the schools have played each other 102 times, every season dating back to 1945. Michigan holds a 67–30–5 edge and has outscored the Spartans 2296 to 1238. The Spartans won in 2008 and 2009, marking their first back-to-back victories over Michigan since a three-game winning streak from 1965 to 1967.

Fielding Yost's "Point-A-Minute" Michigan Teams

From 1901 until 1923, and again in the 1925–26 season, Fielding H. Yost coached some of the most successful Michigan football teams in history. He finished with a career record of 165–29–10, including 56 consecutive games without a loss from 1901 to 1905 and a 49–0 victory over Stanford in the first Rose Bowl game in 1902. Those teams were known as the "Point-A-Minute" teams because of their ability to score a lot of points. In those five seasons, Michigan outscored its opponents 2821 to 42, or an average of 50 to 1 per game.

Michigan won six national championships under Yost in 1901, 1902, 1903, 1904, 1918 and 1923. In those days, there was no clear-cut national champion and other schools claimed national titles in those seasons as well.

The Little Brown Jug

A simple water jug is at the center of the oldest trophy game in college football history. In 1903, Michigan took a 28-game winning streak to Minneapolis to play Minnesota, which entered the game 10–0. Michigan coach Fielding Yost was not confident that Minnesota would provide water for his players, so he instructed a team manager to buy a five-gallon water jug at a local store. The game ended in a 6–6 tie, and in Michigan's haste to return home, the jug remained in Minneapolis. Minnesota equipment manager Oscar Munson found the jug the following morning and painted on its side, "Michigan Jug—captured by Oscar, October 31, 1903." Yost wrote a letter to the Minnesota athletic department requesting the return of the jug, and Minnesota responded by saying, "If you want it, you'll have to come up and win it." Six years later, Michigan returned to Minnesota and beat the Golden Gophers to win back the jug. Although Minnesota won it eight years in a row from 1934 to 1942, Michigan has won 33 of the past 35 games and holds an edge of 66–22–3 in the battle for the Little Brown Jug.

The Aggies Find Success

In 1913, Michigan Agricultural College had its best season to date. The Aggies posted their first unbeaten and untied season at 7–0 and defeated Michigan for the first time. On October 18 at Ferry Field in Ann Arbor, the Aggies knocked off the Wolverines 12–7 in what was described as a very physical game. In *Spartan Football: 100 Seasons of Gridiron Glory*, the game was described as a "bone-breaking, crunching battle." The book went on to say that starting quarterback Blake Miller was forced to leave the game when Michigan quarterback Tommy Hughitt "jumped on Blake's neck with both knees. Blake, unconscious for three hours at a nearby hospital, returned to the team the following Tuesday."

A New Stadium in East Lansing

A new steel-and-concrete facility was unveiled in 1923 after years of playing at Old College Field. Built at a cost of $160,000, the new stadium had a capacity of 14,000 and had its first game in 1923 when Michigan Agricultural College defeated Lake Forest from Illinois 21–6 in front of 7000 fans. The stadium was officially dedicated the following season when the Spartans lost to Michigan 7–0. The stadium was named Macklin Field in 1935 in honor of former Aggies football coach John Macklin, who had a 29–5 record from 1911 to 1915. In 1957, the upper decks were constructed, and the name was changed to Spartan Stadium, and it had a seating capacity of 75,005 as of the 2010 season.

The Big House

Michigan Stadium opened on October 1, 1927, and the Wolverines defeated Ohio Wesleyan 33–0. The vision of former football coach and athletic director Fielding H. Yost, Michigan Stadium had a capacity of 84,401 when it opened. In 1956, the capacity was increased to 101,001, and the first crowd of more than 100,000 showed up on October 6 to watch Michigan State defeat the Wolverines 9–0. As Michigan led the nation in annual attendance in the latter part of the 20th century, Michigan Stadium become known simply as "The Big House." Capacity peaked at 107,501 from 1998 to 2007, and in 2010, it was 106,201 after renovations.

Since its inaugural season, more than 35 million fans have attended games at Michigan Stadium.

And One

It is no coincidence that capacity at Michigan Stadium always ends with the digit of one, so one would say, "a crowd of 106 thousand, two hundred and one." The one was designated as a Michigan tradition in 1956 to honor athletic director Fritz Crisler, whose Michigan football teams had a record of 71–16–3 from 1938 to 1947. The only mystery that remains is the location of Crisler's seat.

Starting at Center, Mr. President

Gerald R. Ford made a name for himself while playing football at Grand Rapids South High School, and he ended up at the University of Michigan, where he started at center and also played defense. The Wolverines were undefeated national champions in 1932 and 1933 when Ford was a sophomore and junior, but in 1934, Ford's senior season, they won only one game. Ford was named the most valuable player on the 1934 team and turned down offers to play professionally for the Detroit Lions and the Green Bay Packers. He went on to coach boxing and football at Yale University as he waited to gain entry into law school. It was the right choice—in 1974, Ford succeeded Richard Nixon to become the 38th president of the United States. Michigan eventually retired uniform number 48 in Ford's honor.

Michigan's Winged Helmets

Football fans across the country can easily identify the University of Michigan when they see the historic winged helmets, which were introduced in 1938 when Fritz Crisler arrived at the school after coaching at Princeton. The University of Michigan's football team had previously worn black helmets, but Crisler wanted to add a little color to them and make them more useful. The maize-and-blue winged pattern was designed so the players would be able to recognize each other on the field. It was essentially the same helmet Princeton used while Crisler was there. The Wolverines wore the winged helmets for the first time in the 1938 season opener against Michigan State. Michigan won 14–0 with sophomore Paul Kromer scoring twice, and a tradition was born.

Old 98

Michigan had many star football players in the first half of the 20th century, but its first Heisman Trophy winner was halfback Tom Harmon, known as "Old 98" because he wore jersey number 98.

Harmon, a passing and running threat and a regular on defense, got his first taste of college football in 1938. However, it was in 1939 that he became a star. He rushed for 884 yards on 130 carries (6.8 yards per attempt) and scored 13 touchdowns. He also completed 37 of 94 passes for 538 yards and six touchdowns, though he did throw eight interceptions. As a senior in 1940, Harmon won the Heisman Trophy, even though his season may have fallen short of his 1939 season statistically. He rushed for 852 yards on 191 carries (4.46 yards per carry) and scored 14 touchdowns, and he was 43-for-94 passing for 506 yards with seven touchdowns and 11 interceptions.

Harmon remained in the public eye for many years after his playing career ended. He served as a pilot in World War II, married film star Elyse Knox and became one of the nation's top sports broadcasters and directors. His son, Mark Harmon, is a former UCLA quarterback and a film star, while his daughter, Kristin, married musician Ricky Nelson, the son of the famous television couple Ozzie and Harriet Nelson.

Back-to-back National Titles for Michigan

Michigan won 25 consecutive games from November 2, 1946, until October 8, 1949, when the Wolverines lost to Army 21–7. During that span, the Wolverines won back-to-back national titles in 1947 and 1948, though there was some controversy surrounding the 1947 crown. Undefeated Michigan had finished number two behind Notre Dame in the final Associated Press poll, but after the Wolverines throttled Southern California 49–0 in the Rose Bowl, an unprecedented post-bowl vote was taken. Michigan was voted number one over the Fighting Irish, sparking a debate about having a one-game matchup to decide the national champion. The Wolverines were led by the "Mad Magicians," tailback Bob Chappius, wingback Bump Elliott, quarterback Howard Yerges and fullback Jack Weisenburger. Three, four or even five men would handle the ball on a typical play, confusing the defenses. The Wolverines ran 180 plays from seven different formations.

Fritz Crisler had coached the Wolverines in 1947, and when former standout quarterback Bennie Oosterbaan took over in 1948, the winning streak continued. However, because no teams were allowed to play in the Rose Bowl in back-to-back years, Michigan was ineligible to play in that bowl despite another undefeated season.

Michigan, which had been ranked fourth, moved to number one after a 28–0 victory over third-ranked Northwestern in the fourth week of the regular season for its third consecutive shutout. After giving up 34 total points in two games—still winning both—the Wolverines slipped to number two, but they finished with shutouts of Navy and Indiana and had a 13–3 victory over Ohio State to wrap up their second consecutive national title.

"Biggie" Munn

As the second half of the 20th century unfolded, Michigan State College, as it had been known since 1925, became the dominant college football program in the state. The primary reason for the success was its coach, Clarence "Biggie" Munn, who led the Spartans from 1947 until 1953. The Spartans were 54–9–2 under Munn, including back-to-back unbeaten 9–0 seasons in 1951 and 1952.

Munn came to Michigan State after one season at Syracuse, and his debut with the Spartans was not a good one. The University of Michigan defeated the Spartans 55–0 in the 1947 season opener, but Michigan State would lose just one more game that season en route to a 7–2 record. It was the beginning of an incredible turnaround for the program. Today, Munn is remembered on the East Lansing campus—the hockey facility is called Munn Arena.

National Champions

Michigan State flirted with the national championship in 1951 by winning nine consecutive games to run its winning streak to 15. Included in the season were victories over the University of Michigan 25–0 and Notre Dame 35–0, and Michigan State finished number two in both the Associated Press and United Press International final polls.

It set the stage for a memorable 1952 season when the Spartans had their second consecutive undefeated season and won the first football national championship in school history. The Spartans steamrolled through nine opponents, and the team was rewarded as six players received all-American honors: guard Frank Kush, halfback Don McAuliffe, center Dick Tamburo, end Ellis Duckett Jr., quarterback Tom Yewcic and halfback Jim Ellis.

A New Conference

The success continued into the 1953 season, and that in itself was a monumental season. Michigan State joined the Big Ten Conference, and in its first season it won the league championship. Michigan State extended its winning streak to 28 games before losing to Purdue 6–0, but that was the only loss all season for the Spartans, who finished 8–1, including 5–1 in the Big Ten—sharing the title with Illinois. It earned Michigan State a spot in the Rose Bowl, and the Spartans responded with a 28–20 victory over UCLA to finish the season 9–1. The "Pony Backfield" was Michigan State's answer to Notre Dame's "Four Horsemen," and those Spartans were halfback Billy Wells, fullback Evan Slonac, halfback Leroy Bolden and quarterback Tom Yewcic. It would be the final game in the stellar coaching career of Munn, who stepped down as coach to take over as the athletic director, a job he held for 18 years.

In 1955, the school became known as Michigan State University, and the football team was prospering. For the first eight years of the 1950s, the Spartans were a combined 62–12, including a 3–6 record in 1954. Munn was named the national coach of the year by the American Football Coaches Association.

"Duffy"

There could not have been many tougher college football jobs in the state at the time than succeeding "Biggie" Munn, but Hugh "Duffy" Daugherty took the challenge. Daugherty had been a member of Munn's staff at Syracuse in 1946, and he came to Michigan State and served as line coach for the Spartans. He took over as head coach prior to the 1954 season but was not immediately successful. Michigan State was 3–6 in its first season under Daugherty but rebounded in 1955 to go 8–1, including 5–1 in the Big Ten, to earn a spot in the Rose Bowl for the second time in three years. Again, the Spartans came back from Pasadena with a victory as they defeated UCLA 17–14. Muskegon native Earl Morrall was the Spartans' all-American quarterback as he threw for 941 yards and five touchdowns.

Daugherty coached at Michigan State through the 1972 season, and he was inducted into the College Football Hall of Fame in 1984. He finished with a career record of 109–69–5 at Michigan State.

The Spartans' Unlikeliest Hero

Dave Kaiser would not likely have been anyone's best bet to be the hero for Michigan State in the 1956 Rose Bowl, but that's exactly what happened. Kaiser had left Notre Dame after one season because he didn't get much playing time, and he ended up at Michigan State. An end, Kaiser had attempted two field goals during the season for Michigan State and missed both, so nobody could have suspected he would provide some late-game heroics.

With the score tied 14–14, Michigan State had the ball deep in UCLA territory, and it was expected that Jerry Planutis would be called in to try the game-winning field goal. But Planutis had missed twice earlier in the game, so Daugherty turned to the inexperienced Kaiser, who made the 41-yard field goal with just seven seconds left in the game. "I wasn't sure I made it until the official near me raised his arms, and then (team captain) Buck Nystrom swarmed all over me," Kaiser said in *Michigan State Football: They Are Spartans*. Kaiser later told the *Lansing State Journal*, "It's amazing how many people still remember that kick. People seem to remember where they were when that happened, like they do when JFK was shot."

Glory Again for Michigan State

While the Spartans followed that memorable Rose Bowl with more successful seasons, they were not able to get back into the national championship picture or return to the Rose Bowl until the mid-1960s. In 1965, Michigan State had one of its most memorable seasons. Led by a stellar defense that included end Charles "Bubba" Smith and linebacker George Webster, Michigan State posted a 10–0 regular season for its first outright Big Ten Conference championship. The Spartans were 7–0 in conference play and added non-conference victories over UCLA, Penn State and Notre Dame. That set up a rematch with UCLA in the Rose Bowl, but after two earlier postseason victories over the Bruins, UCLA responded with a 14–12 victory to spoil Michigan State's perfect season.

Despite the loss, Michigan State earned a share of the national championship. The Spartans were number one in the final United Press International poll and number two in the Associated Press poll.

The 10–10 Tie

With several of its top starts returning, big things were expected of Michigan State in 1966, and the Spartans did not disappoint. Michigan State rolled through the first nine games of its schedule, setting up a huge game with Notre Dame in the season finale. Notre Dame was unbeaten and ranked number one, Michigan State was unbeaten and ranked number two, and the game at Spartan Stadium was billed as the "Game of the Century." Michigan State built a 10–0 lead on a touchdown by Regis Cavender and a field goal by barefoot kicker Dick Kenney, but all that did was set the stage for one of the most controversial finishes in the history of college football.

Notre Dame roared back to tie the game at 10–10. With 1:10 left in the fourth quarter, Notre Dame had the ball on its 30-yard line, but coach Ara Parseghian decided to run out the clock and settle for the tie instead of trying to win the game. Parseghian explained his decision in *Sports Illustrated* by saying, "We'd fought hard to come back and tie it up. After all that, I didn't want to risk giving it to them cheap. They get reckless and it could cost them the game. I wasn't going to do a jackass thing like that at this point."

The decision paid off for Notre Dame, which overwhelmed University of Southern California 51–0 the following week and ended up winning the national championship, while Michigan State and its 9–0–1 record was number two.

Bo and the Biggest Upset

While Michigan State was earning national acclaim in the 1950s and 1960s, Michigan was taking a back seat to the Spartans. After their national championship in 1948, Michigan won Big Ten titles in 1940 and 1950 but didn't win another until 1964, although they did get a pair of wins in the Rose Bowl in 1950 and 1964. Under coach Bump Elliott, the Wolverines were a combined 51–42–2 overall and 32–34–2 in the Big Ten from 1958–68.

The final game of Elliott's coaching career at Michigan was an embarrassing 50–14 loss to hated rival Ohio State. Athletic director Don Canham decided to remove Elliott as coach and make him an associate athletic director, and hire 39-year-old Glenn "Bo" Schembechler to coach the Wolverines. Schembechler had coached the previous six seasons at Miami (Ohio) University, and he had been an assistant coach at Ohio State under Buckeyes coach Woody Hayes.

Michigan won its first two games under Schembechler, beating Vanderbilt 42–14 and Washington 45–7. However, losses in two of the next three games put a damper on Schembechler, especially because one of those losses came in East Lansing against Michigan State. But Michigan followed with four consecutive victories, setting up a conference championship game with Hayes and Ohio State, ranked number one and called the greatest team in the history of college football. Michigan already had a spot in the Rose Bowl wrapped up because Ohio State had played in it the year before and could not play again because of the no-repeat rule. After a 50–14 thumping the previous season, it appeared that Michigan had little chance to beat the Buckeyes, and a spot in the Rose Bowl would have to be good enough. Years later, safety Tom Curtis told annarbor.com, "We wanted to go to the Rose Bowl because we were Big Ten champions, not as Ohio State's replacement."

In what will always be remembered as one of the greatest upsets in school history, the Wolverines defeated Ohio State 24–12.

It was the first game in a heated rivalry between Schembechler and his mentor, Hayes. Although they kept great respect for each other, both wanted to beat the other more than anyone else. Michigan had earned its spot in the Rose Bowl, but the day before the big game, Schembechler suffered a heart attack and missed the game because he was in the hospital. Michigan lost to USC 10–3.

The Ten-Year War

For 10 years, from 1969 to 1978, Schembechler's Michigan teams and Hayes' Ohio State teams met in the regular-season finale with the Big Ten championship or a Rose Bowl bid—or both—on the line every time. The teams traded victories the first four years, and in the fifth year, Michigan tied Ohio State 10–10 in Ann Arbor. They were co-champions, and the deadlock did nothing to break the conference tie and decide which team would play in the Rose Bowl. Michigan star quarterback Dennis Franklin injured his shoulder in the game and was doubtful to play in the Rose Bowl, and a vote was taken by Big Ten athletic directors to decide the conference's representative in the big game. They voted in favor of Ohio State, which infuriated Schembechler and Michigan, who felt they had outplayed the Buckeyes and earned the right to play in the game. Many believed that the athletic directors bypassed Michigan because of Franklin's injury, thus thinking that Ohio State had a better chance to win the game. Ohio State traveled to Pasadena and defeated USC 42–21.

Ohio State won each of the next two meetings with the Wolverines before Michigan reeled off three in a row—the final three games of the 10-year rivalry between Schembechler and Hayes.

To measure the respect each man had for the other, consider the following quotes: "If 'Bo' is not a winner, I never saw one and I should know. He beat me the last three games we played. We've fought and quarreled for years but we're great friends," Hayes said in *The Lantern* in 1986. In the book *Bo*, written by Schembechler and Mitch Albom, Schembechler said, "There was plenty to criticize about Woody Hayes. His methods were tough, his temper was, at times, unforgivable. And, unless you knew him or played for him, it is hard to explain why you *liked* being around the guy. But you didn't just like it, you loved it. He was simply fascinating."

Hayes' coaching career came to a sudden end after the 1978 season when he was fired for slugging an opposing player during the Gator Bowl. Schembechler finished with a 5–4–1 record against Hayes in what is known today as "The Ten-Year War."

Roses for the Spartans

Since the arrival of Schembechler at Michigan, Michigan State and the rest of the Big Ten Conference had tasted little success. The Big Ten was known as "The Big Two and the Little Eight," and the results did not give anyone reason to think differently. However, after more than 20 years from its last Rose Bowl, Michigan State won the Big Ten championship in 1987 and earned a trip to Pasadena to play in the Rose Bowl.

The Spartans were 8–2–1 in the regular season and 7–0–1 in the Big Ten, including a 17–11 victory over Michigan. The Spartans lost to Notre Dame and Florida State in the second and third games of the season, but got things rolling with a 19–14 victory over Iowa in the next game. The stars of the team were halfback Lorenzo White and linebacker Percy Snow. White, who remained the all-time leading rusher in school history with 4887 yards prior to the 2010 season, had rushed for a school-record 292 yards on 56 carries in his final home game at Spartan Stadium. However, in his final minutes with the Spartans, he was more of an onlooker. After carrying the football 35 times in the first three and a half quarters, Spartans coach George Perles rested White in the final minutes of the Rose Bowl.

Perles turned to Blake Ezor, who carried the ball on six consecutive plays to set up a game-winning field goal by John Langeloh to beat USC 20–17. "All day long, they'd been looking at Lorenzo, trying to stop him from cutting back against the grain," Perles told the *Los Angeles Times*. "Then we send Blake (Ezor) in, and he's a ripper. He goes straight at them, and it presents a totally different problem to the defense." Snow, meanwhile, was named the MVP of the Rose Bowl with 17 unassisted tackles.

Finally, Bo Wins the Rose Bowl

Although Schembechler's coaching reputation was growing across the country, the one thing he was criticized for was his lack of success in bowl games. Under Schembechler, Michigan lost the Rose Bowl in 1970, 1972, 1977, 1978 and 1979. Additionally, Michigan lost the 1976 Orange Bowl to Oklahoma and the December 1979 Gator Bowl to North Carolina after the Big Ten decided to allow its teams to play in a bowl game other than the Rose Bowl. So Schembechler was 0–5 in the Rose Bowl and 0–7 in all bowls when the Wolverines played Washington in the Rose Bowl on January 1, 1981.

Although Washington dominated the game early, Butch Woolfolk rushed for 182 yards on 26 carries and scored on a six-yard touchdown run in the second quarter as Michigan defeated the Huskies 23–6.

After that initial bowl victory, Schembechler became more successful in the postseason. Michigan won in three of Schembechler's final five bowl games, including the 1988 Rose Bowl against USC, and he finished with an overall record of 194–48–5 at Michigan, including 143–24–3 in the Big Ten Conference and 5–12 in bowl games.

Two for the Heisman Trophy

In the 1990s, Michigan had two of the 10 Heisman Trophy winners, the first of whom was wide receiver Desmond Howard. Howard, an electrifying runner, led Michigan to three Big Ten Conference championships in three years and won the Heisman Trophy in 1991.

Howard appeared on the Heisman radar in a game against Notre Dame in 1991. On a game-deciding four-and-inches play, quarterback Elvis Grbac threw a pass to Howard, who fully extended himself on a dive in the back of the end zone to haul in the 25-yard touchdown pass as the Wolverines beat Notre Dame 24–14. Howard then put the artistic touch on the Heisman during the Ohio State game when he returned a punt 93 yards for a touchdown and, after he found the end zone, he suddenly struck a pose identical to the one that stands atop the Heisman Trophy. The award was his.

Charles Woodson was a rarity: he is the only primarily defensive player to win the Heisman Trophy. Woodson was a defensive back with a penchant for making big plays. He became a starter in just his second game at Michigan and started 34 games in a row before leaving for the NFL after winning the Heisman Trophy (and several other awards) in 1997 as a junior.

Michigan—National Champs Again!

Led by Heisman Trophy winner Charles Woodson, Michigan rolled through its 1997 schedule undefeated and edged Washington State 21–16 in the Rose Bowl to finish number one in the coaches' poll as national champion. The Wolverines were a bit miffed when Nebraska, which was number two after the regular season, vaulted over Michigan to number one in the Associated Press poll after beating third-place Tennessee 42–17 in the Orange Bowl. Michigan didn't win the national title the easy way, either, as six of its final seven opponents, including the final four, each were ranked in the top 25 at the time of the games. The Wolverines opened with a 27–3 victory over Colorado and added victories over Baylor, Notre Dame, Indiana, Northwestern, Iowa, Michigan State and Minnesota. At 8–0, Michigan was ranked fourth and had a game against third-ranked Penn State. Michigan overwhelmed the Nittany Lions 34–8 and was rewarded with a number one ranking the following week. Michigan then visited Wisconsin and beat the Badgers 26–16 to set up a clash with Ohio State at Michigan Stadium. Michigan, coached by Lloyd Carr, maintained its spot at the top with a 20–14 victory over the Buckeyes and then defeated Washington State in the Rose Bowl to wrap up a 12–0 season.

Clockgate

In maybe the most controversial of all University of Michigan–Michigan State games, a 2001 game played at Spartan Stadium still draws the ire of Wolverines fans. Michigan had a 24–20 lead with Michigan State driving in the final minute of the fourth quarter. On second and goal with 17 seconds left, Michigan State quarterback Jeff Smoker rolled to the right and ran two yards to the one-yard line, but did not go out of bounds to stop the clock. The Spartans frantically lined up to spike the ball and stop the clock, and when they did, one second showed on the clock. Michigan coaches and players argued that clock operator Bob Stehlin stopped the clock too soon and time should have run out. With one second left, Smoker threw a touchdown pass in the back of the end zone to T.J. Duckett, setting off a wild celebration after a 26–24 victory. This is one Michigan–Michigan State game that will be debated for years.

Goodbye, Bo

Even as his health deteriorated, Bo Schembechler maintained his office at Schembechler Hall and was never far from the Michigan program. On November 19, 2006, Schembechler went to a local television studio to tape his weekly football program. Just a month earlier, he had collapsed as he left the same television studio, and had a pacemaker and defibrillator implanted in his chest. This time, when Schembechler collapsed again, doctors could not save his life, and he died on that Friday afternoon at age 77.

The timing of Schembechler's death was ironic, coming one day before the annual Michigan–Ohio State game—the biggest rivalry game of his career. And this one was the biggest of the biggest of the Michigan–Ohio State games: both teams had 11–0 records, and Ohio State was ranked first and Michigan was ranked second. The game was played in Columbus, Ohio, and Ohio State prevailed 42–39.

A Fantastic Finale

Lloyd Carr was the head football coach at Michigan from 1995 through 2007, and he could not have picked a much better way to go out than the way he did. Carr, who had coached Michigan to the 1997 national championship, won five Big Ten titles at Michigan and was named the national coach of the year in 1997. He had announced in November that 2007 would be his final season as coach of the Wolverines, so there was plenty of emotion on January 1, 2008, when Michigan played Florida in the Capital One Bowl in Orlando, Florida. The Wolverines were ready. Quarterback Chad Henne passed for 373 yards and three touchdowns, while Mike Hart ran for 129 yards and two touchdowns as unranked Michigan upset ninth-ranked Florida 41–35 for their first bowl victory since 2003. At the end of the game, the Michigan players doused Carr with water, and then they put him on their shoulders and carried him to midfield. "It's extremely meaningful on a personal level," Carr said. "But the reason it's meaningful is because I can be in that locker room with the guys that did it. Our coaches put together a great game plan, our players executed. Of course, we were big so-called underdogs. To come up with that kind of effort and to find a way to win means that we have some memories that we're all going to be able to celebrate for years to come."

Basketball Beginnings

College basketball was much slower than college football to come into its own, but its roots are nearly as old. Basketball at Michigan State, then known as Michigan Agricultural College, dates back to 1898, but for the first half of the 20th century, the scores were low and the game was not as popular as football. Michigan State did not join the Big Ten Conference for basketball until 1950.

Michigan did not field a team until it played five games in 1909, and the Wolverines did not have another men's basketball team until the 1918–19 season. Michigan tasted success in the 1920s, winning the Big Ten Conference title three times under coach E.J. Mather and another time under coach George Veenker, but there would be just one more league title—1948 under coach Osborn Cowles—prior to the 1963–64 season. Bennie Oosterman, Michigan's talented football quarterback, was also a two-time all-American in basketball in 1927–28, though Michigan's first all-American basketball player was center Richard Doyle in 1926.

The Spartans Hit the Big Time

In 1957, Michigan State made it to the NCAA tournament for the first time, and it was a memorable event. The Spartans, under coach Forddy Anderson, made it to the Final Four in the 23-team tournament. Michigan State opened with an 85–83 victory over Notre Dame in the Mideast Region semifinals and defeated Kentucky 80–68 in the region finals. That set up a semifinal game against North Carolina, and it was one for the ages.

North Carolina was 30–0 and ranked number one, but the Spartans made it a classic. Amazingly, the score was 29–29 at halftime and 58–58 at the end of regulation. The Spartans had a chance to win in the first overtime. Holding a two-point lead with seconds to play, a Michigan State player missed a free throw, and Pete Brennan of North Carolina grabbed the rebound and went coast-to-coast for a game-tying rebound. North Carolina, which eventually won the national title, finally defeated Michigan State 74–70 in three overtimes.

The Cazzie Years

In the middle of the 1960s, Michigan had one of the top men's basketball programs in the country.

The Wolverines of coach Dave Strack won three consecutive Big Ten Conference titles in 1964, 1965 and 1966, as well as NCAA regional championships in 1964 and 1965. The player at the center of all that success was Cazzie Russell, a guard out of Chicago. Russell rewrote the Michigan record book as he finished his career with 2163 points. He held single-season scoring records in each of his three seasons at Michigan, and his career average of 27.1 points per game, remains the best in school history, as does his single-season average of 30.8 in the 1965–66 season. Russell could do it all, and he quickly became not only one of the most popular college basketball players in Michigan, but also one of the most popular in the country. With Russell at guard, two-time all-American Bill Buntin at center, Oliver Darden and Larry "Trigger" Tregoning at forward and George Pomey at guard, the Wolverines were a force.

It started in the 1963–64 season with Russell's arrival. The Wolverines went 23–5 overall and 11–3 in the Big Ten and made the NCAA tournament for the second time in school history (the 1947–48 team was the first). The Wolverines opened in the Mideast Regional and edged Loyola-Illinois 84–80 before beating Ohio 69–57 for the regional championship. In the Final Four, Michigan lost to Duke 91–80 in the national semifinals.

Michigan was ranked number one by both the Associated Press and the coaches' poll in 1964–65 with a 24–4 record and 13–1 in the Big Ten. The Wolverines went to the NCAA tournament and won the Mideast Regional, beating Dayton 98–71 in the first game and Vanderbilt 87–85 in the championship game. The Wolverines then opened the Final Four with a 93–76 victory over Princeton, setting up a championship game against UCLA and legendary coach John Wooden. All-American Gail Goodrich and the Bruins were too much for Michigan and beat the Wolverines 91–80 to win the national championship.

After that season, Buntin left for the NBA and was drafted with the third overall pick by the Detroit Pistons. Three years later, Buntin died after suffering a heart attack while playing in a pickup basketball game.

In Russell's senior season, it was obvious the team missed Buntin, but Michigan still managed to go 18–8 and 11–3 in the Big Ten. Michigan beat Western Kentucky 80–79 in the Mideast Regional semifinals before losing to Kentucky 84–29 in the regional final. Russell was named the NCAA Player of the Year and was the number one pick in the NBA draft.

The House That Cazzie Built

When Russell came to Michigan, the basketball games were played on a removable court at Yost Field House. However, the enthusiasm shown by the fans toward Russell led to the construction of a basketball arena called Crisler Arena, although to many, Crisler Arena really is the "House That Cazzie Built."

One Win Away

With Cazzie Russell gone from the college scene, basketball success was less common in Michigan, both in Ann Arbor and in East Lansing. Rudy Tomjanovich gave Michigan an all-American performer in the late 1960s, but "Rudy T." did not bring any Big Ten championships to the program. At the same time, Michigan State had an all-American player in Ralph Simpson, but he, too, failed to deliver a championship to his program. But things changed dramatically in the middle of the 1970s, starting with an amazing run in the NCAA tournament by Michigan in 1976.

The Wolverines of coach Johnny Orr finished the regular season ranked ninth after going 21–6 in the regular season and 14–4 in the Big Ten. Led by guard Ricky Green and center Phil Hubbard, the Wolverines rolled through the NCAA tournament, beating Wichita State and Notre Dame to get to the West Regional final, where Michigan topped Missouri 95–88. In the Final Four for the first time in

11 years, Michigan defeated Rutgers 84–70 to earn a chance to play for the national championship. In the Wolverines' way was Indiana, which not only was undefeated, but had beaten Michigan twice during the regular season. Michigan was not able to prevent Indiana and coach Bob Knight from completing a perfect season with a national championship as the Hoosiers scored an 86–68 victory over Michigan.

Magic in East Lansing

With Michigan on top of the basketball world in the state, there was a high school player at Lansing Everett High School who was gaining a lot of attention. His name was Earvin "Magic" Johnson. Fred Stabley Jr., a sports writer for the *Lansing State Journal*, first called the 15-year-old Magic because he thought Johnson had magical skills after watching the sophomore score 36 points, grab 18 rebounds and hand out 16 assists in one game. As a senior, Johnson led Everett to a 27–1 record and the Class A state championship, and he was easily the hottest college prospect around. UCLA and Indiana, among others, were offering scholarships, and Michigan, a year removed from its runner-up finish in the NCAA tournament, wanted him, too. But Johnson, who stood 6-foot-8, wanted to play point guard, and that didn't seem possible, especially at Michigan, his original preferred destination. Michigan State coach Jud Heathcote promised Johnson that he could have a shot at playing point guard, and

Magic decided that he would stay home in Lansing and attend school at Michigan State. The announcement of his decision drew statewide media attention.

Heathcote had just completed his first season at Michigan State, and Johnson really didn't know him that well. Plus, the Spartans had finished the 1976–77 season with a 10–17 record, so it's easy to see why this wasn't a slam-dunk decision for Magic. But he made more of an impact than anyone could have imagined. In their first year with Johnson, the Spartans finished 25–5, including 15–3 in the Big Ten, and were ranked fourth in the final Associated Press poll and fifth in the coaches' poll. Michigan State defeated Providence and Western Kentucky in the NCAA tournament before losing to eventual national champion Kentucky 52–49. Johnson averaged 17.0 points, 7.9 rebounds and 7.4 assists per game as a freshman. He was putting Michigan State on the national basketball map.

A Magical Season

The expectations were high in East Lansing after the success of the previous season, and the Spartans did not disappoint. Michigan State began the season ranked seventh in the Associated Press poll and rose to number one by midseason. A couple of losses dropped them to fourteenth, and by the time the NCAA tournament rolled around, Michigan State was 21–6, including 13–5 for a three-way tie for first place in the Big Ten. The play of Johnson at point guard made everyone else around him a better player, including Greg Kelser, who had been there for two seasons prior to Johnson's arrival and became an all-American player as a senior. Kelser was the leading scorer on the team at 18.8 points and 8.7 rebounds per game, while Johnson checked in at 17.1 points, 7.3 rebounds and 8.4 assists per game.

Michigan State opened the NCAA tournament with an easy 95–64 victory over Lamar, and the Spartans followed that with an 87–71 victory over Louisiana State University. In the regional final, the Spartans defeated Notre Dame 80–68 to earn their first berth in the Final Four since 1957. In the national semifinals, Michigan State destroyed Penn 101–67, setting up a game against undefeated and top-ranked Indiana State and its star player, Larry Bird, for the national championship. Johnson and Bird didn't like each other, even though they didn't know each other. They both wanted the same thing, and they stood in each other's way. The game was billed as "The Magic Man vs. The Bird."

On March 26, 1979, Michigan State and Indiana State elevated college basketball in the eyes of the nation. An estimated 20 million people watched the game on television, not only the largest audience ever for a college basketball game but also a record that would stand for more than three decades. With a capacity crowd of 15,410 watching at the Events Center in Salt Lake City, Utah, Michigan State stormed to a 37–28 lead at halftime.

Indiana State got within six points in the second half but could get no closer as the Spartans won the national championship with a 75–64 victory. Johnson, who scored 24 points, was named the MVP of the tournament, while Bird had 19 points on 7-for-21 shooting with 13 rebounds and five steals.

It was only the beginning of the Magic–Bird rivalry. Magic went on to lead the Los Angeles Lakers to the NBA championship five times in the 1980s, while Bird's Boston Celtics won three titles. And, eventually, their rivalry turned into a close friendship.

"A Michigan Man Will Coach Michigan"

Bill Frieder took over as coach of the Michigan basketball team in 1981 and had some success. In 1984, the Wolverines won the National Invitational Tournament, but Michigan and its fans wanted to win the big one—the NCAA tournament. The 1988–89 team gave its fans some hope by going 21–6 in the regular season. But, on the eve of the NCAA tournament, Frieder threw a bombshell onto the lap of Bo Schembechler, the legendary football coach who also was the team's athletic director. Frieder told Schembechler that he had received an offer to coach at Arizona State, and he planned to take the job and leave Michigan as soon as the NCAA tournament ended. Schembechler was furious and immediately fired Frieder. "A Michigan man will coach Michigan," were

Schembechler's legendary words, and as far as he was concerned, Frieder was no longer a Michigan man, he was an Arizona State man. Schembechler named Steve Fisher, an assistant coach under Frieder, as the interim coach for the duration of the NCAA tournament.

A Pair of Clutch Free Throws

The 1989 Wolverines had five players who would play in the NBA: Rumeal Robinson, Glen Rice, Loy Vaught, Terry Mills and Sean Higgins, but it was the overall excellent play of Rice and the clutch free-throw shooting of Robinson that helped Michigan win the national title with an 80–79 victory over Seton Hall in overtime. Rice had a chance to win it in overtime, but his last-second shot missed. In overtime, Seton Hall grabbed a quick three-point lead, and Mills cut it to 79–78 with just less than a minute to play. After a missed shot by Seton Hall star John Morton, Michigan grabbed the rebound with 12 seconds to play. Robinson wanted the ball. "I've been coming down and passing the ball and hiding a lot on last-second shots," Robinson said in *Sports Illustrated*. "This time, I wanted it to be me. I was going to hit it if it was a free throw or not." Robinson was not a great free-throw shooter (he made just 64.2 percent of his shots during the season), but he was fouled in the lane with three seconds to play and he sank both free throws to give Michigan a one-point lead with three seconds to play. The Wolverines held on to win the national championship.

The Fab Five

While Fisher, who had been retained as coach, was never able to win another national championship at Michigan, he recruited one of the most talented classes in the history of college basketball. High school stars Chris Webber and Jalen Rose, both from Michigan, signed to play for the Wolverines, as did Juwan Howard of Chicago and Ray Jackson and Jimmy King, both from Texas. Webber, Rose and Howard were immediate starters, while King and Jackson joined the starting lineup later in the season.

Finally, on February 9, 1992, all five freshmen started for the first time as the Wolverines played Notre Dame in South Bend, Indiana. Rose wrote the following in *Dime* magazine: "I remember that we were struggling a bit and right before the (Notre Dame) game, Coach Fisher's dad passed away. We wanted to win so bad for him. He was real emotional and I remember him being like, 'It's time to start the Fab 5.'" Michigan won the game 74–65 to improve to 14–5, and went on to earn a spot in the regional finals.

Michigan, which by this time had adopted the saying, "Shock the World," didn't let the bright lights of the Final Four become a problem, and the Wolverines topped Cincinnati 76–72 to earn a spot in the national championship game against tournament-tested Duke. However, Duke's experience was too much for the Wolverines, as the Blue Devils won the national title with a 71–51 victory.

Obviously, Michigan had all five freshmen back for their sophomore seasons in 1992–93, and it seemed as if nothing less than a national championship would be satisfactory. As the team landed back in the Final Four, Michigan matched up with Kentucky, the number one seed from the Southeast Regional, and scored an 81–78 victory to earn a return to the national championship game.

This time, it was North Carolina awaiting the Wolverines, and the game was much closer than the Duke game from the previous year. But the game is remembered more for a blunder made by Webber. With North Carolina leading 73–71, Webber grabbed a defensive rebound with 19 seconds to play. Webber dribbled down and, while in front of the Michigan bench, he signaled for a timeout with 11 seconds to play. However, Michigan had used all of its timeouts, so Michigan was charged with a technical foul, and North Carolina went on to win the game 77–71. Webber, who finished with 23 points and 11 rebounds, was crushed. "I just called the timeout and that probably cost us the game," he said.

Webber left Michigan for the NBA after his sophomore season, and he was the number one overall pick in the NBA draft. Rose and Howard left

Michigan after their junior seasons, while Jackson and King remained at Michigan for all four seasons.

Unfortunately, the story of the Fab Five had a tough ending. Michigan had to forfeit both runner-up finishes after the NCAA ruled that team booster Ed Martin had improperly made payments to players, including Webber, to launder money from an illegal gambling operation. Michigan also forfeited the 1997 NIT championship and the 1998 Big Ten Conference tournament championship because of the scandal, which also implicated players Robert Traylor, Maurice Taylor and Louis Bullock, who were not a part of the Fab Five era.

The Flintstones

Later in the 1990s, Michigan State had its own special group of players, but they weren't all freshmen starters at the same time. Mateen Cleaves, Morris Peterson and Charlie Bell all played high school basketball in Flint, about 50 miles from East Lansing, and they became known as "The Flintstones." Antonio Smith was a fourth member of the group, but he graduated in 1999—one year before the Spartans won the national championship.

The Spartans defeated Eastern Michigan and Princeton before losing to North Carolina in the regional semifinals of the NCAA tournament in 1998, and Cleaves, Bell and Peterson were the top three scorers on the team. The next season, Michigan State went 33–5 as Peterson led the team in scoring with 13.5 points per game, while Cleaves was next with 11.7. The outright Big Ten champs (15–1) rolled through the region with victories over Mount St. Mary's, Mississippi, Oklahoma and Kentucky to gain a spot in the Final Four for the first time since the Magic Johnson years. But Duke's tournament experience proved to be too much for Michigan State as the Blue Devils scored a 68–62 victory in the national semifinals.

Cleaves and Peterson were seniors in the 1999–2000 season, and their focus was evident after the near miss of the previous season. They went 26–7 in the regular season with four players averaging in double figures: Peterson (16.8), Cleaves (12.1), Bell, who was a junior (11.5), and Andre Hutson (10.2). Michigan State won all four of its games in the regional by double figures, putting it in the Final Four, where it faced Big Ten opponent Wisconsin. Michigan State took care of the Badgers 53–41 to land a spot in the national championship game against Florida. At the RCA Dome in Indianapolis, Michigan State defeated Florida 89–76 to win the second national championship in school history.

Cleaves was named the MVP of the tournament, and he was selected in the first round of the NBA draft by the Detroit Pistons, although he never lived up to expectations in the NBA. Peterson, too, was a first-round pick as he was taken by the Toronto Raptors, and he spent the first seven seasons of his career in Toronto. He averaged a career-high 16.8 points per game in the 2005–06 season and had scoring averages in double digits in four seasons. Bell stayed at Michigan State for his senior year and went back to the Final Four with the Spartans, who lost to Arizona 80–61.

The Izzone

Tom Izzo had taken over as coach for Jud Heathcote prior to the 1995–96 season, and with all the success Michigan State enjoyed in the late 1990s, he became very popular in East Lansing and the rest of the state—except, of course, Ann Arbor. Students seated in the section behind the bench declared the area, "The Izzone," and wore shirts with that saying.

Izzo, who grew up in Iron Mountain, Michigan, developed a reputation for having his teams ready to make a run in the NCAA tournament. In his first 15 seasons at Michigan State, Izzo had a record of 364–146, including 174–76 in the Big Ten. The Spartans made the NCAA tournament 13 years in a row through the 2009–10 season, and in that time they lost in the first round just three times and in the second round only once. Michigan State had six appearances in the Final Four in those 13 years, including a runner-up finish in 2009 when the national championship game was played at Ford Field in Detroit.

Izzo had a few opportunities to move on to the NBA as a coach, but he decided to stay in East Lansing. Early in the 21st century, Izzo had extensive talks with the Atlanta Hawks, and in the summer of 2010 he was offered the chance to coach the Cleveland Cavaliers. After nine agonizing days during which the media speculated Izzo's future, Izzo turned down the Cavaliers, saying he was "going to be at Michigan State for life."

Chapter Six

And In This Corner...

It seems as if boxing's glory days are over, and most of the top bouts are held in Las Vegas or Atlantic City. But it wasn't always that way.

Michigan has a rich boxing history, starting with legendary former champion Joe Louis to current star Floyd Mayweather Jr. The state has also hosted several championship bouts, including those by Louis and Sugar Ray Robinson, and Detroit's Kronk Gym was once one of the most famous training sites in America.

The Michigan Assassin

Although he mainly fought out of Butte, Montana, Stanley Ketchel never abandoned his Michigan ties. Known as the "Michigan Assassin," he was the state's first real boxing star. Ketchel was born in Grand Rapids, but left the state as a teenager after the deaths of his parents. He hopped a boxcar and took it to Montana, where, with no training, he began a boxing career.

In 2003, *The Ring* magazine ranked the top 100 punchers of all time, and Ketchel came in sixth, ahead of such powerful boxers as Jack Dempsey, George Foreman, Rocky Marciano and Mike Tyson. He is considered one of the greatest middleweights of all time, yet he fought the legendary Jack Johnson for the heavyweight title in 1909. Johnson won on a 12th-round knockout.

Ketchel had a record of 51–4–4 (with 48 knockouts) when he was murdered at the age of 24. He was eating breakfast in Conway, Missouri, when he was shot in the back by Walter Dipley, who believed that his wife, Goldie Smith, was far too interested in the boxing champion. Ketchel was taken by train to a hospital in Springfield, Missouri, where he died on October 15, 1910.

In 1959, Ketchel was a member of the fifth class of inductees into the Michigan Sports Hall of Fame, and he was just the second boxer to be inducted.

The Brown Bomber

Joe Louis is so ingrained in the history of Detroit that the home of the Detroit Red Wings is named Joe Louis Arena and there's a statue of Joe Louis' fist outside Cobo Hall in downtown Detroit. That's because Louis was much more than a champion heavyweight boxer who some consider to be the best ever—Louis was also a genuine American hero, and his achievements helped ease race relations in the United States.

Louis, also known as "The Brown Bomber," was born in Alabama, and his family moved to Detroit when he was 10. He immediately became involved in boxing, and at age 20, he won the Golden Gloves competition as a light heavyweight, after which he turned professional. Louis, who had a 50–4 record as an amateur, steamrolled his opponents, beating former heavyweight champion Primo Carnera in front of a crowd of 62,000 at Yankee Stadium, and knocking out former heavyweight champion Max Baer in the fourth round. That set the stage for about against Max Schmeling, another former champion. Schmeling pulled off the upset, knocking out Louis in the 12th round and returning to his native Germany a national hero.

Germany and the United States were at odds. Schmeling was supposed to face American heavyweight champion James J. Braddock, and some feared that if Schmeling won the title, he would not defend it, thus neutralizing the heavyweight belt. Louis stepped in to face Braddock, and, after being knocked down in the first round, he knocked out Braddock in the eighth round to win the heavyweight title and become the first black heavyweight champion since Jack Johnson. It set up a tempting rematch with Schmeling that had obvious political implications. Two weeks prior to the fight, Louis visited President Franklin Delano Roosevelt, who said to the champ: "Joe, we're depending on those muscles for America."

On June 22, 1938, Louis defended his title against Schmeling in Yankee Stadium in New York. The world was watching, as were 70,000 people at the ballpark in the Bronx—and reportedly up to 100 million people were listening on the radio. The event seemed to touch all corners of America—the white South and the black and Jewish communities, as well as Nazi Germany.

The fight lasted 124 seconds. John Kieran of the *New York Times* wrote the following after the fight:

> *Well, of all things! It's on and it's over. Just as Joe promised. He stepped in and started a lightning attack. Lefts and rights—Bang! Bang! Bang! Schmeling reeled into the ropes on the first-base side of the ring and clung like a shipwrecked soldier to a lifeline. Swaying on the ropes, Max peered out in a bewildered manner. He pushed himself off, and Louis struck like dark lightning again. A ripping left and a smashing right. The right was the crusher. Schmeling went down. He was up again and then, under another fusillade, down again. Once more, and barely able to stand, and then down for the third and final time.*

Louis retained his heavyweight championship title, and America had a national hero—a black one at that. He defended his title 25 times and won by knockout in 22 of them. Two of his title defenses were held in Detroit: an 11th-round knockout of

Bob Pastor at Briggs Stadium on September 20, 1939, and a 13th-round technical knockout of Abe Simon at Olympia Stadium on March 21, 1941.

Louis retired from boxing on March 1, 1949, but he had to come out of retirement to pay back some $1 million that he owed the International Revenue Service. He lost his title on September 27, 1950, when Ezzard Charles won on a 15-round decision. Louis finished his career with a record of 68–3, including 54 knockouts.

While Louis will always be regarded as one of the best boxers of all time, the victory over Schmeling was the signature moment of his career. Heywood Broun wrote the following in the *New York American*:

> *One hundred years from now some historian may theorize, in a footnote at least, that the decline of Nazi prestige began with a left hook delivered by a former unskilled automotive worker who had never studied the policies of Neville Chamberlain and had no opinion whatever in regard to the situation in Czechoslovakia.... And possibly there could be a further footnote. It was known that Schmeling regarded himself as a Nazi symbol. It is not known whether Joe Louis consciously regards himself as a representative of his race and as one under dedication to advance its prestige. I can't remember that he has ever said anything about it. But*

*that may have been in his heart when he
exploded the Nordic myth with a bombing glove.*

Louis died on April 12, 1981, at age 66. And
a sidenote—Louis was not Joe's last name. He was
born Joseph Louis Barrow. There are various theo-
ries as to why Louis dropped the surname Barrow,
but the most logical is that, while filling out a form
for one of his first amateur fights, there was not
enough room for his last name, so he just used the
name Joe Louis. And from that, a legend grew.

Bringing the Fight to Detroit

Detroit hosted many top-level fights over the years,
including the first heavyweight title fight of the
1900s. On April 6, 1900, James J. Jefferies knocked
out Jack Finnegan in the first round to retain the
heavyweight title at the Cadillac Athletic Club in
Detroit. The knockout came at 55 seconds, and it
remained the quickest knockout in a heavyweight
title fight in boxing history until George Foreman
knocked out Jose Roman in 50 seconds in 1973.

Sugar Ray Robinson, a Detroit-born boxer, and
Jake LaMotta, known as the subject in the movie
Raging Bull, fought each other five times between
1943 and 1951, and the first two of those bouts
were held at Olympia Stadium in Detroit. In the
first fight, on February 5, 1943, LaMotta used his
trademark bull-rushing style to overpower
Robinson for a 10-round unanimous decision.
Three weeks later, on February 26, 1943, Robinson

and LaMotta had a rematch, again at Olympia, and this time Robinson used left jabs and uppercuts to win on a unanimous decision. Known as the best pound-for-pound boxer of all time, he finished 4–1 in his fights with LaMotta.

Robinson, born Walker Smith Jr., first used the name Ray Robinson when he substituted for a fighter with that name, as he did not have the proper certificate to fight under his own name. Robinson finished his professional career with an incredible record of 175–19–6 with 109 knockouts.

On March 7, 1951, Ezzard Charles successfully defended his heavyweight title by beating Jersey Joe Walcott on a decision at Olympia Stadium. It was the second of four fights between Charles and Walcott.

The most recent heavyweight title fight was held on June 12, 1981, appropriately at Joe Louis Arena. Larry Holmes successfully defended his title with a third-round technical knockout of former champion Leon Spinks. The fight was held two months to the day after the death of Louis.

The Motor City's "Hitman"

The greatest boxer to come out of Detroit's famed Kronk Gym, run by trainer Emanual Steward, was Thomas "Hitman" Hearns, who won titles in six different weight divisions during his career, which began in 1977. After winning his first 28 professional bouts, Hearns had a fight with Pipino Cuevas for the World Boxing Association welterweight title on August 2, 1980, at Cobo Arena in Detroit. The hometown star won on a second-round technical knockout of Cuevas for his first professional title. Hearns went on to win titles as a light middleweight, middleweight, light heavyweight, super middleweight and cruiserweight.

Hearns finished his career with a record of 61–5–1 with 48 knockouts. He had two epic fights with Sugar Ray Leonard, losing on a technical knockout in the 14th round in 1981 and fighting to a draw in 1989 while knocking Leonard down in the third and 11th rounds. In 1985, Hearns and Marvin Hagler staged a bruising three-round fight in which Hagler won in the third round on a technical knockout. *The Ring* magazine, the bible of boxing, called the opening three minutes "one of the greatest first rounds of all time," and called the fight "the most electrifying eight minutes ever."

A Boxing Family

The name Mayweather has been synonymous with boxing in Grand Rapids for decades, but it wasn't until Floyd Mayweather Jr. came along that it became a household name. Mayweather is the son of former welterweight contender Floyd Mayweather and the nephew of former WBC super featherweight champion and IBO light welterweight champion Roger Mayweather and former IBO super featherweight champion Jeff Mayweather. But Floyd "Money" Mayweather Jr. surpassed them all by going undefeated in his first 41 pro fights, winning the WBC super featherweight title, the WBC lightweight title, the IBF and WBC middleweight titles and the WBC light middleweight title. He fought four times in his hometown of Grand Rapids and once at Cobo Arena in Detroit.

Among Mayweather's biggest wins was a 12-round decision over Oscar de la Hoya on May 5, 2007, in a fight that produced more than $180 million in revenue. Mayweather also has wins over Angel Manfredy, Diego Corrales, Jesus Chavez, Arturo Gatti and Zab Judah. He beat Sugar Shane Mosley in a unanimous decision on May 1, 2010, and was hopeful of a matchup with WBO welterweight champion Manny Pacquiao.

Chapter Seven

The Game of Summer

Michigan residents have never let the snow and cold of winter dampen their passion for golf. There are nearly 1000 golf courses in Michigan, and men, women and children are drawn to them in the spring, summer and fall. Maybe it's the limited number of months to play the game, or maybe it's the beautiful Michigan summers, but more than likely it's the game itself that appeals to so many in the state.

Oakland Hills—"The Monster"

Walter Hagen was its first club professional, Jack Nicklaus and Arnold Palmer won major senior tournaments there and Ben Hogan gave Oakland Hills Country Club in Bloomfield Hills its nickname. "I am glad I brought this course, this monster, to its knees," Hogan said after winning the 1951 U.S. Open. And the South Course at Oakland Hills would be known from then on as "The Monster."

The South Course opened on July 13, 1918, and was designed by Donald Ross, the leading architect of golf courses in his day. The North Course opened in 1924 as a second course for club members. Hagen, who had 11 major titles among his 45 PGA Tour victories from 1914–36, was the club professional from 1918 until the early 1920s.

The South Course has hosted six U.S. Opens, three PGA Championships, two U.S. Senior Opens, the U.S. Men's Amateur and the U.S. Women's Amateur, the Western Open, the Carling World Open and the Ryder Cup. But it is the 1951 U.S. Open that remains the signature major tournament of "The Monster."

Hogan entered just five tournaments in 1951 and won three of them, including the Masters with a then-record 274. He entered the U.S. Open as the defending champion but started with a 76 in the first round. After 54 holes, Hogan was two strokes off the pace, but he shot a 67, including a 32 on the back nine, to win the title by two strokes over Clayton Heafner.

Another magical moment at Oakland Hills came during the 1972 PGA Championship, won by Gary Player. Player had a three-stroke lead on the back nine but had it sliced to one with back-to-back bogeys. But on the 16th hole, Player hit a fantastic shot over the trees, and he had to sprint up the fairway to see that the ball had settled on the green three feet from the pin. Player made the putt for a birdie to secure the victory.

Augusta's First Champion

By the time Horton Smith retired from golf, he had become the answer to a couple of trivia questions. Smith, the club professional at the Detroit Golf Club from 1946 until his death in 1963, won the first Masters tournament at Augusta National Golf Club in 1934, and he won it again in 1936. He was also the last player to defeat the great Bobby Jones in match play before Jones retired in 1930. And Smith is credited with being the first professional to use a sand wedge in competition. He used one in 1930, but it had a concave face and was soon banned. Later, Gene Sarazan invented the sand wedge as it is known today.

The Greatest Amateur

There are many things that are subject to debate when it comes to sports, but in the state of Michigan, there is no debate about this—Chuck Kocsis is the greatest amateur golfer in history. The Golf Association of Michigan voted that honor upon Kocsis in 1999, and Kocsis was among the first class of golfers inducted into the Michigan Golf Hall of Fame. He won the Michigan Amateur six times, the Michigan Open three times and was an individual NCAA champion while at the University of Michigan. He was also a member of three U.S.

Walker Cup teams and was successful in golf's major championships as an amateur. Kocsis was the low amateur twice at the Masters and twice at the U.S. Open. He finished second in the 1956 U.S. Amateur and was runner-up at the 1937 Western Amateur.

The Mother Hubbard Open

Under normal circumstances, the Michigan Golf Classic that was held in 1969 would be nothing more than a footnote in golf history. But the first PGA Tour event held at the Shenandoah Country Club on Walnut Lake Road in West Bloomfield is remembered by some as the Mother Hubbard Open—because the cash cupboard was bare at the end of the tournament.

The tournament was the brainchild of Marshall Chambers, the club chairman, Jim Dewling, a Birmingham caddymaster at the time, and club pro Ray Maguire. In 1968, the Birmingham Country Club hosted the U.S. Women's Amateur, and after seeing the success of the tournament, the three went in search of a place to hold a PGA Tour event in Detroit. The PGA was already visiting Michigan with the Buick Open in Grand Blanc, a suburb of Flint, but Detroit had been without a Tour stop since the Motor City Open ended in 1962. But there were problems.

Word got out that Shenandoah was not on par with other courses that hosted PGA Tour events, and the Michigan Golf Classic was being held the same weekend as the World Series of Golf, so just three of the top 20 money winners entered the tournament. The weather didn't cooperate, so ticket sales were low, and the men behind the tournament, including Phil Lachman, the owner of a local trophy store, were not prepared financially for such a situation. Dewling retold the story to *Michigan Golfer* magazine.

"At one o'clock on Sunday afternoon, Mr. Lachman says, 'Jimmy, let's go for a cart ride,'" Dewling said. "He said I seemed to be the only one around there who knew what went on. We drove out to a spot where there was no one around, and he told me there was no money and they weren't going to pay the purse. I think, 'Wow, this is wild.' He said Chambers hadn't come up with any money, and the pro-am didn't generate any money. We drove back to the clubhouse, and he got in his car and left. When presentation time came, everyone disappeared."

Eventually, the PGA Tour paid all the players. The total purse was $100,000, with $20,000 going to the winner, Larry Ziegler.

Brothers Win PGA Tour Events in Same Year

Brothers Dave and Mike Hill of Jackson are two of the most successful professional golfers to come from the state of Michigan. Both are members of the Michigan Sports Hall of Fame. But in 1972, the Hill brothers did something pretty remarkable—each of them won a PGA Tour event. Dave, who won 13 PGA Tour events, got things started by winning the Monsanto Open on April 16 in Pensacola, Florida. Later, on November 5, Mike captured the San Antonio Texas Open for the second of his three PGA Tour titles. He won by two strokes over Lee Trevino, who ironically would become his partner on the PGA Senior Tour as the duo would pair to win five Liberty Mutual Legends of Golf titles.

Dave was the more successful player on the PGA Tour. In addition to his 13 titles (four in the Memphis Open), he won the Vardon Trophy in 1969 for the lowest scoring average on the tour and played for the United States three times in the Ryder Cup. Dave was also runner-up in the 1969 U.S. Open, and he won six times on the PGA Senior Tour. Mike, meanwhile, had more success on the Senior Tour with 18 titles, and he was the leading money winner in 1991.

Mr. Accuracy

Calvin Peete didn't pick up a golf club until he was 23 years old, had an impaired left arm and dropped out of school when he was 15. Not exactly a typical future professional golfer, not to mention that Peete, born in Detroit in 1949, was an African American man. But, he became a consistent winner on the PGA Tour with 12 wins, including in 1982 when he became the first black golfer to win four PGA Tour events in one year.

A fall out of a cherry tree when he was 12 left Peete with a shattered left elbow, which never fully regained its normal range of motion. However, some believe that helped him keep his drives in the fairway as it helped him with his timing, and he earned the title of "Mr. Accuracy."

"Calvin had beautiful rhythm and tempo," golf instructor Butch Harmon said on www.thesandtrap. com. "And because his elbow was fused, he was able to create a swing path that allowed him to return the club to the same position at impact."

Peete won his first PGA Tour event in 1979 when he captured the Milwaukee Open, and his four victories in 1982 helped him finish second in scoring average (70.33) and fourth on the money list with $318,470. Three years later, he picked up his biggest win when he took the Tournament Players Championship.

Peete was the first black golfer to play on two Ryder Cup teams, the second black golfer to win more than $100,000 in a season, and he also won the Vardon Trophy in 1984 for the lowest scoring average on the PGA Tour, at 70.56. He won more than $2 million during his professional career. Obviously, Peete's race is irrelevant in earning him a place in golf history.

A Beer-Drinkers' Tournament

To refer to the 17th hole at the Warwick Hills Golf and Country Club in Grand Blanc simply as a par 3 doesn't tell the whole story—at least, not when the Buick Open was around. The Buick Open was held at Warwick Hills from 1958 until 1969 and again from 1977 through 2009, and it was the 17th hole that became legendary. Fans would gather around the green and create chants for the golfers, and they would indulge in some adult beverages at the same time. "This is a great tournament to play in; it's a beer-drinkers' tournament," golf pro John Daly said. In fact, the 17th green would become known as the second-largest outdoor cocktail party in the world, apparently giving way to the Florida–Georgia college football game.

The PGA Tour organizers decided not to hold the Tour again in Grand Blanc after the 2009 event, which made for an interesting final day at the 17th hole. One man dressed in a lime green bodysuit emblazoned with the words "Save the Open." Although entertaining, the gimmick didn't work, and the Buick Open did not return to Grand Blanc in 2010.

A Place for Future Champions

Since 1971, Point O' Woods Golf and Country Club in Benton Harbor has been home to the Western Amateur, one of the top amateur golf tournaments in the United States. The Western Amateur first took place in 1899 and has been held every year since then except for 1918 (World War I) and 1943 to 1945 (World War II). While

at Point O' Woods, Hal Sutton and Justin Leonard
have been back-to-back winners. Phil Mickelson
took the title in 1991, and Tiger Woods was the
1994 champion.

Chapter Eight

They Were as Good as Gold

Detroit has a unique distinction when it comes to the Olympic Games—the largest city in Michigan has bid to host the Summer Olympics Games seven times, and it has been denied every time. No other city has tried as many times as Detroit without being selected as the host city at least once.

However, Michigan is the home of many successful Olympians who have been decorated with gold, silver and bronze medals in various sports. The following are some of the best.

Midnight Express

Eddie Tolan, known as the "Midnight Express," was discovered because of his speed while playing football and running track at Detroit Cass Tech High School, where he was a two-time sprint state champion as a sophomore. He added two more titles as a senior at the National Interscholastic Championships, and that set the stage for a stellar career at the University of Michigan, where he set a world record of 9.5 seconds in the 100-yard dash in 1929. He went on to win the national title in the 220-yard dash and took four national Amateur Athletic Union sprint titles. That led to the 1932 Olympic Games in Los Angeles, and Tolan, who stood 5 feet, 7 inches and weighed just 145 pounds, won the 100-yard dash in a world record–tying 10.3 seconds and added gold in the 200-yard dash in an Olympic-record 21.2 seconds. In the process, he became the first black athlete to win two Olympic gold medals. Ironically, the two previous runners to win gold in both the 100- and 200-yard dashes were University of Michigan athletes: Wisconsin native Archie Hahn in 1904 and Detroit native Ralph Craig in 1912.

During his career, Tolan won 300 races and lost just seven.

Mr. Weightlifting

There is a very good reason that Detroit native Norbert Schemansky received the nickname of "Mr. Weightlifting"—he was the first weightlifter to win four medals in the Olympic Games. In 1948, he won the silver medal as a heavyweight, and in 1952, he won the gold as a middle heavyweight. After missing the 1956 Games because of a back injury, Schemansky returned to win bronze medals in 1960 and 1964 as a heavyweight. He had personal-bests of 415 pounds in the press competition and 445 pounds in the clean and jerk, and he won nine AAU national championships.

In 2005, the International Weightlifting Federation called Schemansky the "best weightlifter of 100 years."

King Makes a Splash

Micki King, a native of Pontiac, was one of the feel-good stories of the 1972 Summer Olympics. At the 1968 Games, King, one of the top female divers in the world, was third in the springboard when she hit the board and fractured her wrist on the 10th and final dive, and she finished fourth, out of the medals. A University of Michigan graduate, she didn't let adversity get her down. At the 1972 Olympics, King, who held the rank of captain in the U.S. Air Force, was in third place with three dives remaining, but she vaulted from third to first to claim the gold medal. The following year, she was named diving coach at the U.S. Air Force Academy—the first female to become a faculty member at a military academy in the United States.

Gold, Silver and Bronze

Birmingham native Sheila Young was one of the stars of the 1976 Winter Olympic Games when she won a gold, a silver and a bronze in women's speed skating. It made her the first U.S. athlete to win three medals in a single Winter Olympics. Twelve years earlier, she had competed in the U.S. National

Championships, and she made her Olympic debut in 1972, finishing fourth in the 500 meters. A year later, Young pulled off a unique double when she won the world sprint championships in both cycling and speed skating, making her the first athlete of the 20th century to become world champion in two sports at the same time. At the 1976 Innsbruck Winter Olympics, Young won gold in the 500 meters, silver in the 1500 meters and bronze in the 1000 meters.

A First for the United States

Hazel Park native Steve Fraser made American wrestling history at the 1984 Olympics Games in Los Angeles, winning the men's light heavyweight title in Greco-Roman wrestling to become the first American to win a gold medal in that sport. He won five matches en route to the title, including a 4–1 decision over three-time world champion Frank Andersson of Sweden. It is considered one of the most historic matches in U.S. wrestling history. In the gold-medal match, Fraser won on criteria after tying Ilia Matei of Romania 1–1. The criteria was last point recorded, and Fraser scored the final point after trailing 1–0.

"One of the Greatest Paddlers of Our Lifetime"

Greg Barton is the most decorated American canoe/kayak athlete of all time. Growing up on a pig farm in Homer, Barton became the first American to win an Olympic gold medal in kayaking when he triumphed in the 1000 meters during the 1988 Summer Olympics in Seoul, Korea. Then he teamed with Norman Bellingham to win the men's 1000-meter pairs and earn a second gold. Barton also won the bronze medal in the 1000 meters in 1984 and repeated with another bronze in the 1000 meters in 1992. "Greg is one of the greatest paddlers of our lifetime," David Yarborough, executive director of USA Canoe/ Kayak, said on canoekayak.com.

In all, Barton won four world championships and 50 national titles.

Chapter Nine

Honorable Mention

Bowling Capital of the World

It's a title that surely is debated in many cities, but certainly for a while, Detroit was right in there with St. Louis and Milwaukee as the Bowling Capital of the World. And for good reason. Detroit was home to the legendary beer teams, most notably the Stroh's team that won the 1934 American Bowling Congress (ABC) tournament and five national match game titles between 1934 and 1945. The captain of the team was Joe Norris, who retired as the man with the most total pinfall (123,770) in the history of the ABC tournament. Norris competed in the event for 71 years and had an average score of 193 during that span. He also was the youngest ABC-sanctioned bowler to roll a 300 game at age 19 (a record since broken many times), and he was the oldest to do so at age 86 (also since broken).

The beer teams would travel from city to city with home-and-home challenges, and the Stroh's team was one of the best. Fred Wolf of Detroit loved the home-and-home travel matches. "We might leave their town 400 pins down, but we'd be smiling because we knew we'd get them on our home alleys," Wolf told the *Detroit News* in 1978. After Norris left the Stroh's team, Buzz Fazio took over as captain, and Stroh's won the ABC team championship three years in a row, in 1952, 1953 and 1954.

Detroit also is one of several Michigan cities that have been home to many events on the Professional Bowlers Association Tour.

Wonderful Women of the Lanes

There are many facts and figures that explain why Marion Ladewig of Grand Rapids is considered one of the greatest female bowlers of all time. She was the first female inducted into the Michigan Sports Hall of Fame, and nationally known Detroit columnist Joe Falls once compared her to baseball legend Babe Ruth and hockey legend Gordie Howe.

Ladewig's stats also back up the claims. Nine times between 1950 and 1963, she was voted the Bowler of the Year by the Bowling Writers Association of America. She also won the first of five Women's U.S. Open titles in 1949 and finished her career with eight championships and was runner-up twice. Ladewig won the inaugural Professional Women's Bowling Association championship in 1960, and she was named Woman Bowler of the Century by *Bowlers Journal International* in 2000.

She is a member of the Women's Sports Foundation Hall of Fame and the Women's Professional Bowling Hall of Fame.

Later in the 20th century, Aleta (Rzepecki) Sill of Dearborn became the face of women's bowling in Michigan. Sill was the first women's bowler to reach $1 million in career earnings, a feat she accomplished in October 1999. A left-hander, she had 31 career professional titles, including the Triple Crown of women's bowling: the U.S. Open, the WIBC/USBC Queens and the Sam's Town Invitational. Sill won her first professional title at the age of 19.

Racing on the River

The American Powerboat Association Gold Cup is the oldest active trophy in all of motorsports, dating back to 1904, and making it older than the prestigious Indianapolis 500, which originated in 1911.

The Detroit River has been a consistent host to the running of the Gold Cup, and hydroplane racing became big in Detroit in 1915 when designer Christopher Columbus Smith of the Chris Craft boat company won the Gold Cup with *Miss Detroit*. The race was held in Manhasset Bay, New York, and is one of the most heralded Gold Cup races of all time. After the planned driver could not be located, Johnny Milot volunteered to drive *Miss Detroit*. However, he became seasick during the first heat and riding mechanic Jack Beebe was forced to take over, piloting the boat to victory. The win allowed Detroit to host the event the following year.

For the next nine years, the Gold Cup was held in Detroit, with Detroit boats winning five of those titles. The city hosted the event 17 times from 1937 until 1986, and beginning in 1990, the event was held in Detroit every year except 2008, when the race was cancelled because of high winds.

In 1955, Detroit driver Lee Schoenith, driving *Gale V,* became the first winner to average more than 100 miles per hour when he posted a winning speed of 102.5 miles per hour.

The City of Champions

Detroit was known as the City of Champions in 1935, and it was a well-earned name. That year, the Tigers won the World Series, the Lions won the NFL title, the Red Wings won the Stanley Cup, Detroit native Joe Louis was among the best heavyweight boxers in the world, boat racer Gar Wood of Detroit won the Harmsworth Trophy and the Stroh's bowling team of Detroit won the world match game title.

Soccer's World Cup Comes to Pontiac

In 1994, the Silverdome in Pontiac was one of nine sites in the United States to host the World Cup—and it was the only venue that featured indoor action. In fact, the match on June 18 between the United States and Switzerland, which ended in a 1–1 tie, was the first World Cup game to be played indoors. Grass was grown by Michigan State University and planted inside the domed stadium to make it playable for soccer. The Silverdome also hosted games between Romania and Switzerland, Sweden and Russia and Brazil and Sweden. Brazil eventually won the World Cup at the Rose Bowl in California.

Detroit's Professional Soccer Teams

The Detroit Express was the first professional soccer team to call Detroit home. The Express played in the North American Soccer League from 1978 to 1980 and played their home games at the Silverdome in Pontiac. British star Trevor Francis led the team with 22 goals and 10 assists in 19 games as the Express won the Central Division of the American Conference with a record of 20–10. Because of poor attendance, the team was moved to Washington, DC, but Detroit businessman Sonny Van Arnem retained the name Express and put a team in the American Soccer League in 1981. The Express won the league championship in 1982 but folded after the 1983 season.

Detroit also had the Rockers, who played in the National Professional Soccer League from 1990 to 2001. The Rockers played their home games at Joe Louis Arena, Cobo Arena, The Palace of Auburn Hills and Compuware Arena. Led by star player Andy Chapman, they won the league title in 1992 but folded when the league ceased operation in 2001. Around the same time, the Detroit Safari, originally known as the Neon, played at The Palace of Auburn Hills in the Continental Indoor Soccer League. With Chapman, who left the Rockers to play for and manage the Neon, they led the league in attendance in their first season in 1994. The team folded in 1997 when the league closed.

Additionally, Detroit had the Detroit Lightning for one season in 1979 in the Major Indoor Soccer League before the franchise became the Kansas City Comets, and the Detroit Ignition played in the MISL in 2006–07 and 2007–08 at Compuware Arena.

The Annual Yacht Race

In 1925, members of the Bayview Yacht Club decided to have a race up the Michigan shoreline— a distance of 236 statute miles. Today, it is known as the Port Huron to Mackinac Race, and every summer, yachtsmen battle waves and winds in one of only two freshwater yacht races in the world. Measuring by number of participants, the Port Huron to Mackinac Race is the largest long-distance race on fresh water.

Boats are measured to determine handicaps, with the fastest boat not receiving a time allowance. The race typically begins on a Saturday afternoon with the first boats arriving at Mackinac Island early Monday.

The Brow, The Barber, Mo Cheese and Gus

Michigan is one of the most passionate sports states in America, and it isn't because of its teams or its athletes. It's the fans that make sports in Michigan, and over the years, four of them became well known to the athletes and the other fans.

The first was Gus Sinaris, a heavyset man who was a staple at the Detroit Pistons games at Cobo Arena during the 1960s and 1970s. Sinaris, a former boxer with a flat nose who also worked as a vendor at Tiger Stadium and Olympia Stadium, would rise from his seat in the upper deck and do a silly dance that entertained fans during some of the Pistons' most dismal performances. The scoreboard at Cobo would implore, "Gus, Dance For Us," and he never disappointed.

While Gus was too far away from the court to disrupt anything, Leon "The Barber" Bradley sat courtside and never kept his mouth shut. Bradley was at every game during the Pistons' glory years of the late 1980s through the 1990s, and his sharp tongue would be directed at opposing players whenever possible. After Bradley's death, former Celtics great Bill Walton wrote, "It doesn't seem like a Detroit game anymore without the late Leon the Barber. A man with the most venomous tongue in league history. A fan who it's best to stay out of his sights, but a man everyone truly loved."

Joe Diroff was a retired seventh-grade math teacher with big, bushy eyebrows. He attended all the games—the Tigers, the Lions, the Pistons and the Red Wings—and he never sat down. "The Brow," as he was known, would simply walk around the venue as a self-proclaimed cheerleader, except that his cheers were very unorthodox and he would bring props. One of his most famous routines included a plastic ketchup bottle and a plastic mustard bottle. He would hoist the ketchup bottle in the air and yell, "You know why the Yankees can't catch up?" And then he would grab the mustard bottle and answer his own question, "Because they can't cut the mustard." Diroff would often be the only fan to greet the Detroit teams at the airport when they arrived in the middle of the night.

The most recent of the outrageous fans is Scott Stebbins, a fertilizer salesman who is known as "Mo Cheese." He has been a staple at Joe Louis Arena for Red Wings games for nearly 20 years. He wears a replica of the Stanley Cup on his head and a Red Wings jersey with the name Mo Cheese on the back. When there was a break in the action, the Red Wings play the "Curly Shuffle," and Mo runs down from his spot in the standing-room-only section and does his best curly shuffle, to the delight of the crowd.

Yes, the games are the main thing, but fans like these certainly jazz up a game and make attending a sporting event in Michigan a unique experience.

Notes on Sources

Books

Addy, Steve. *Four Decades of Motor City Madness*. Urbana, IL: Sagamore Publishing, 1997.

Bak, Richard. *A Place for Summer: A Narrative History of Tiger Stadium*. Detroit: Wayne State University Press, 1998.

Cohen, Richard. *The University of Michigan Football Scrapbook*. Indianapolis: Bobbs-Merrill, 1978.

Ewald, Dan, Hawkins, Jim, Van Dusen, George. *The Detroit Tigers Encyclopedia*. Champaign: Sports Publishing LLC, 2003.

Falls, Joe. *50 Years of Sportswriting*. Urbana, IL: Sagamore Publishing, 1997.

Fischler, Stan. *Detroit Red Wings: Greatest Moments and Players*. Champaign: Sports Publishing LLC, 2002.

Grinczel, Steve. *Michigan State Football: They Are Spartans*. Mount Pleasant, SC: Arcadia Publishing, 2004.

Hoffman, Ken. *Spartan Football: 100 Seasons of Gridiron Glory*. Urbana, IL: Sagamore Publishing, 1996.

Strother, Shelby. *The NFL Top 40*. New York: Viking, 1988.

Periodicals

Ann Arbor News
Baseball Digest
Detroit Free Press
Detroit News
Lansing State Journal
Los Angeles Times
Michigan Golfer

Ring Magazine
Sports Illustrated
The Sporting News

Websites
www.baseball-reference.com
www.detroitlions.com
www.mgoblue.com
www.msuspartans.com
www.nba.com/pistons
redwings.nhl.com
retrosheet.org
tigers.mlb.com